# Heal Your Ancestral Roots

---

"Anuradha Dayal-Gulati, Ph.D., has written a thoroughly engaging guide to gaining more contentment, fulfillment, and harmony in life. This gem of a book will make an important contribution to the emergence of new energy-based therapies. It is rare to find a guide to the gifts of the Earth, ancestors, and spirit that is so highly informative and heartfully lyrical."

—**Dan Cohen, Ph.D.,** family constellation
facilitator and author of *I Carry Your Heart in
My Heart: Family Constellations in Prison*

"Anu's clear, concise, down-to-earth writing style and easy to follow exercises make her book one of the best for beginners, clients, and practitioners alike. Sharing her step-by-step process, she shows you how to find peace and contentment in your life by connecting to yourself, to your family energy field, to the Earth, and ultimately to the Source of all that is. I wholeheartedly recommend this book."

—**Susan Ulfelder, ND, LMT, BCPP, RDH,**
traditional naturopath, doctor of integrative medicine,
and founder of the Hellinger Institute of DC

"This book seeks to outline an alternative path forward—one that involves healing one's roots and forging a new path. To accomplish this, the book introduces two crucial concepts—family energy fields and flower essences—that complement familiar techniques to address family trauma, like therapy and essential oils."

*"Heal Your Ancestral Roots* offers a thought-provoking option for dealing with family issues, creating a path to a more fulfilling life."

**—BlueInk Review**

"A compelling, spirited guide that aims to help readers understand who they come from."

***—Kirkus Reviews***

# Heal Your Ancestral Roots

## Release the Family Patterns That Hold You Back

Anuradha Dayal-Gulati, Ph.D.

 FINDHORN PRESS

Findhorn Press
One Park Street
Rochester, Vermont 05767
www.findhornpress.com

SUSTAINABLE Certified Sourcing
FORESTRY
INITIATIVE  www.sfiprogram.org
SFI-00854

Text stock is SFI certified

Findhorn Press is a division of Inner Traditions International

**Disclaimer**

The information in this book is given in good faith and is neither intended to diagnose any physical or mental condition nor to serve as a substitute for informed medical advice or care. Please contact your health professional for medical advice and treatment. Neither author nor publisher can be held liable by any person for any loss or damage whatsoever which may arise from the use of this book or any of the information therein.

Stories of individuals have had details altered to protect confidentiality.

Cataloging-in-Publication data for this title is available from the Library of Congress

ISBN 978-1-64411-774-3 (print)
ISBN 978-1-64411-775-0 (ebook)

Printed and bound in the United States by Lake Book Manufacturing, LLC
The text stock is SFI certified. The Sustainable Forestry Initiative * program promotes sustainable forest management.

10 9 8 7 6 5 4 3 2 1

Edited by Jennifer Taylor, Taylor-Editing.com
Text design and layout by Liz Schreiter / Reading List Editorial and Anna-Kristina Larsson
This book was typeset in Kepler Std and Minion Pro

To send correspondence to the author of this book, mail a first-class letter to the author c/o Inner Traditions • Bear & Company, One Park Street, Rochester, VT 05767, USA and we will forward the communication, or contact the author directly at **healyourancestralroots.com**.

*This book is dedicated to my spiritual lineage,
to my ancestors, and to my wonderful and
extraordinary parents—my mother, Pramoda,
and my father, Moni. You are the wind in my sails.
Words cannot do justice to all that
I have received from you.*

# Contents

Preface     11

Introduction: Living Life in Full Bloom     15

    Do You Have the Power to Change Anything?     18

## Part I: Healing My Roots

1   Why Heal Your Roots?     25

    Can You Inherit the Fate of Your Ancestors?     26

    Seeing Patterns     28

    Filling the Void     32

    What Happens When Your Ancestors Fail to Move On?     37

    What to Expect in This Book: The Journey Ahead     40

2   The Power of the Unseen     44

    The Dispensation of Hope     50

    The Arrival of Haripriya     52

    Leaving India     57

3   From Fate to Destiny     63

    Discovering Flower Essences     65

    The Threshold of Life and Death     71

    My Lifeline     73

    Finding My Purpose     75

4   Discovering Family Energy Fields     77

    What Is a Family Constellation?     79

    Whose Emotions Are We Carrying?     83

    Karma: The Law of Cause and Effect     89

# Part II: Healing Tools

**5  Healing with Flower Essences**                                    **95**

How Essences Work                                                      101

Essences of Transformation                                            104

How Long Should You Take Flower Essences For?                         106

**6  How to Honor Your Ancestors**                                    **110**

How to Set Up an Ancestral Altar                                      114

The Power of Prayer                                                   118

Prayers to Release the Past                                          118

Your Ancestors Want to Connect with You Too                          120

How to Do Tarpanam                                                    122

# Part III: Understanding Your Family Energy Field

**7  Rewriting Your Parental Story**                                  **127**

The Debt of Life: Parents Give and Children Receive                  128

How Trauma Affects Your Roots                                        129

Understanding Your Parental Wounds                                   133

Rewriting Your Parental Story                                       137

Releasing Your Unconscious Loyalty to Your Parents                  139

Connecting with Universal Unconditional Love                        145

**8  Parents Give and You Receive**                                  **150**

The Queen of Strengths                                              151

Your Unconscious Blocks to Receiving                                153

Honoring Our Parents                                                160

The Energy of a Mother's Love                                       162

**9  Everyone Belongs in a Family**                                  **170**

Why Does This Happen?                                               173

Our Hidden Legacies                                                176

The Elephants in the Room                                           177

Making Space for Everyone                                          179

## Part IV: The Journey Home

**10 The Path Back to Yourself**    189

Karma and Grace    190

Faith Takes You Beyond Synchronicity    194

The Challenge of Building Faith    196

**11 Connecting with Mother Earth**    202

What Does It Mean to Be Grounded?    206

The Healing Power of Water    209

**12 Let Your Life Blossom**    214

What Does It Mean to Honor Your Life or Yourself?    215

Shifting Your Perspective    215

Self-Care and Self-Compassion    218

Blessings to Blossom    221

Filling the Hole Within    223

**13 The Four Pillars**    230

The Price of Belonging    231

The Path of Transformation    234

Connecting to the Flow of Love and Life    236

From Sight to Insight    238

## Appendices

**A:** Some FAQs on Flower Essences    241

**B:** Flower Essences and Essential Oils    244

**C:** A Starter Kit of Flower Essences    246

**D:** Five Flower Essence Formulas    249

*Formula #1: An Optimism Formula*    249

*Formula #2: Boundaries*    250

*Formula #3: Self-Love and Self-Worth*    251

*Formula #4: Need Direction?*    253

*Formula #5: Letting Go*    254

Glossary                    256

Resources                   275

List of Exercises           277

Acknowledgments             279

Index                       282

About the Author            286

# Preface

Graduate school was a dreary place. As soon as school was out, my husband and I took our backpacks and transported ourselves to wherever the cheapest tickets to an international location took us, which was typically Europe. Those few glorious summers were spent in warm sunshine, filled with fresh bread, ripe tomatoes, and spontaneous friendships. I had married a wanderer—an extroverted, gregarious soul. As we listened to open-air concerts, eating in small towns off the tourist path, and sleeping on ferries to save our meager finances, we met other couples, and sometimes traveled together with them. We would join and leave the groups like waves that came together and then went back out to sea. If my husband had his way, we would have spent our lives crisscrossing the earth with our backpacks. But the summer would end, the money would run out, and doctoral dissertations would loom over us again.

Over the years my husband's wanderlust did not diminish, and I also gave birth to two children who shared their father's love of travel. Each destination we went to was met by them with wonder and delight. But I was changing. Although I participated in the decision of where we would go, as I worked with energy healing—flower essences and family constellations—something in me was shifting. The person who returned was not the one who had left. I became aware that the Universe wanted to guide me to each destination depending on what I needed to learn at that moment. In the past, I had traveled in some ways to escape my daily life; now I traveled to come home to myself. I listened keenly, watched carefully, and gave my ego a rest. This was the journey of my soul. Each experience, person, their story, or the history of the land had a message for me. A larger force was guiding my journey. I became aware of the sacredness of the earth, the universality of our stories, dreams, and aspirations, as well as our challenges. I began to notice everyday angels and light workers who lived in our midst.

With every journey I took, I wanted to bring something back with me, and to experience that feeling of standing in the full expression of myself, fearless, and in alignment with my purpose. Yet, as long as I was entangled, it was hard to do that. I was entangled with my ancestors, stories of colonialism and capitalism and my own stories. Where could I start? Through flower essences and family constellation therapy, I became aware of the forces acting on me and I could loosen the grip of ideas and emotions that up to now held me in their spell.

In graduate school, we had a friend, Joe. A stocky guy with a deep laugh, and eyes that crinkled at the end when he greeted us with his warm smile. He talked endlessly about being in the rat race. He would always say, "Even if you win the race, you're still a rat." We would argue with each other about whether it was possible to stay on this human course of making a living without being a rat! The rat race is about survival. I had a fear that if I took time to listen to my soul, I might drop out of the rat race— and not survive. For a large part of the Indian population, life is about survival—meeting the needs of water, food, and a roof over their heads. But, for a significant part of the American population, too, life is about survival as people work—sometimes even multiple jobs—to pay for food, rent, and health care. How do we shift from surviving to thriving? This is the question that plagued me when I saw poverty and hardship on the streets. The question I struggled with hadn't changed over the years, but the field in which I searched for answers was different. The rat race was all about accomplishments measured in visible indicators, possibly at the expense of one's mental and physical health as well as human connection. And, yet, money and the trappings of power, I discovered, at some point, seemed unrelated to feelings of internal security, abundance, generosity, and self-worth.

When you are in a system and start to question it, you open yourself to experiencing freedom, expansion, and growth. This is the call of your soul! To answer the call of my soul, I had to leave the familiar and known. There were times when I thought I couldn't do it. I would rather slink into oblivion and die unfulfilled than write and share what I had learned. If we don't live with intention and courage, we are likely to find ourselves and our day hijacked by others, including our ancestors.

INTRODUCTION

# Living Life in Full Bloom

*Surrounded by nurturing relationships, working creatively in your zone of genius, you have adequate time for self-care, enjoy effortless awareness of healthy boundaries, and are filled with feelings of gratitude, contentment, fulfillment, inner confidence, and harmony.*

How does that sound? Does that sound like your life? Do you feel that you are living your life in full bloom?

Or do you feel stuck in one or more areas of your life? You know what you want, you even think you know how to get it, but somehow you can't get there. You see your own limitations and blocks but are not able to break through.

The youngest of six, Sally was warm, friendly, and outgoing. She had a job that helped bring in much-needed income and also gave her an opportunity to travel occasionally, which she loved. Although she enjoyed the good pay and the travel, she felt burned out by the demands on her time. When her eldest daughter struggled with health issues, her life began to feel out of control, and getting it back on an even keel seemed even more out of reach. When her department was reorganized, she found herself having to take on more; she finally left her job in frustration. In searching for help and direction, she started reiki, and then other complementary and healing therapies to get the support she needed.

Like Sally, you might have tried several different approaches—such as shifting jobs, moving, cutting what you feel are toxic people out of your life, or even hiring a life coach. You may have tried alternative healing approaches such as acupuncture, meditation, or other modalities, and perhaps, you even felt that things were changing.

Yet, despite starting the journey to healing and to changing things in her life, Sally felt as if some things in her life were "stuck." Her family situation was strained by the time and cost of medical treatments, and her personal relationships with some of her family members left her upset and drained. With both her parents gone, she was now no longer on speaking terms with some of her siblings. She felt helpless—as if no matter what, some things just didn't seem to shift. Do you too feel as if there's a ceiling on life that shows up in different ways?

What if Sally could see that this feeling of "stuckness" may not have originated with her—that its roots extended further back than she thought—to way before her?

The sensation of being stuck is a feeling of being in a situation where things are not changing, despite your efforts. If you look closely, you might notice that behind this is a pattern. Perhaps some of these patterns are obvious to you, but sometimes you may not see them. For instance, you might notice that like you, your parents were disconnected from their siblings or their parents.

Sally's mother had stopped talking with her siblings over a series of misunderstandings a long time before her death. When family stories or anecdotes are narrated over and over again, what's the takeaway of the story? Is there a common thread? Is the key character a victim of incidents that happened in their family, of injustices done to them by someone in the community or extended family? Or is the character a hero? Sally's mother felt she had been taken advantage of by her siblings because she had shouldered the responsibility of taking care of their mother without much financial support from them. Sally too had done the same.

Sometimes, themes reappear in a family for several generations in a row—of financial distress, bankruptcy, business failure, sibling rivalry, divorce, or, conversely, long, happy marriages, good health, extended family sing-alongs, constant bantering, and good humor. You might have always noticed these themes or patterns, thinking little of them, or treating them simply as a coincidence. Or you might have felt the influence of these patterns so strongly that you felt this was fate that you were powerless over. But what if there is more to this feeling of "stuckness" than meets the eye?

What if these patterns of events, experiences, and emotions that repeat in your life and relationships are indicating that something in your life needs healing? What if the source of these patterns is your family—but not as you know it? What if family is not just a nuclear entity with your parents, siblings, or even grandparents, but an energy field that includes those who are no longer alive? Like the backstories of a character in a novel, the experiences of your ancestors affect your life, even if you are unaware of them. This family energy field or family karma tries to keep coming to your attention through the repetition of patterns, events, and emotions. If you look closely, you might even feel that the same patterns and attendant emotions show up again and again through the people who come into your life and the events that repeat, leaving you feeling the same way each time.

If the "stuckness" had no emotions attached to it, you would not feel its burden. The earth is an emotional plane and a karmic energy plane. You feel frustrated tied to a job you dislike, or despair that your family relationships don't work, or sad that your dreams have expired. Perhaps you feel discouraged that there's a ceiling on your prosperity or you keep waiting for your soul mate, leaving each date dispirited and disheartened. You keep a tight lid on feelings of frustration, despair, hopelessness, and anger that keep circling within you, but sometimes these feelings escape, hurting others in their wake.

What if the emotions that keep you prisoner may not be your own? Emotions are the connecting element between two worlds, the physical world you live in and the invisible world that you cannot see.

## Do You Have the Power to Change Anything?

When I started working with Sally, I drew her attention to the patterns I noticed, offering the possibility of her family energy field that was preventing her from achieving what she wanted. Sally then started to talk about her family, and how her older brother died before she was born. No one had ever talked of him. Using some of the exercises outlined in this book, Sally honored his death and her parents and grandparents. In connecting with her ancestors, she started to be able to let go of feelings of resentment and being ignored and invisible in her large family of six siblings. Feelings that her mother too had experienced when she had shouldered the care of her own mother.

Working with the family energy field can bring up a lot of emotions. You may experience a resistance to letting go of the past, of hurts, grievances, shame, the grief of betrayal, heartbreak and so much more. Is there a way to work with them, hear their message, and more importantly recognize that these emotions are carriers from the family energy field? As she started to explore her family history, Sally was able to repair her relationships with her siblings and extended family.

Working with your family energy field, you too can transform these patterns or family karma so that you are no longer burdened by them and condemned to repeat them. You may be the one your ancestors have been waiting for: the one who will bring about healing and repair of the family energy field. When you start to do that, you lift the ceiling on your own life and also for those who may come after you.

Sally found support for her healing journey. She was able to shift the emotions that seemed to grip her so tightly. Using different tools of healing, like flower essences—a form of energy medicine—she was able to create change in her life. While essential oils are widely known and used, flower essences have been around for thousands of years—only rediscovered about a hundred years ago. They are organic, wild-crafted, natural, and safe. In this book, you will learn the key essences that can shift your emotions to create the change you want.

My clients say:

"The essences help remove emotional obstacles and make your life happier and easier."

"Things that seem challenging suddenly feel doable."

"I feel grateful for my life, and I can finally let go of the past."

With the help of flower essences, emotions shift so you can find calmness and inner confidence. Working with your ancestral energy field, you can understand where those emotions originated and how they influence you.

What this book will show you is that the roots of your disconnection did not originate with you. You may try to fill this void by searching for connections with others—friends, family, community, but it leaves you disappointed and unfulfilled. Even if this disconnection did not originate within you, it lives within you. Your ancestors live within you. When they are forgotten, disliked, or disrespected, they cast their shadow in order to be seen. You never release the patterns or feelings of unhappiness, unfulfillment, or disconnection that act as a ceiling on your life. You do not, however, need to know your ancestors to do this work.

You are the flower of your family tree. How do you find the capacity to bloom?

This book shows you the four pillars that help you do that. In addition to connecting with your ancestors, you need to connect with the power of the Universe that supports you. When you are not in alignment with this latent power, you are disconnected from yourself. No matter how much you try, you cannot change this sense of disconnection from outside yourself. To shift your emotions, you also need to connect with the healing energy of the earth—the energy that your ancestors were tied to until not that long ago. The energy that is also available through the power of flowers. When you connect with these sources within you— the healing energy of your ancestors, the earth, and the power that supports and guides, then you can connect with yourself— the fourth pillar—and feel the sanctuary that exists within. Feelings of gratitude, harmony, contentment, love, and connection fill you. Through this process, you recover your self-worth and inner confidence.

Today, Sally is much more connected with her feelings and herself. She feels happier, grateful, and more connected with her family. She spends time in nature, which nurtures her soul. The journey to her ancestors and herself found its expression in the work she does. She helps people express themselves by working as a voice coach to professionals and teaching theatre to young children.

When you restore your connection to yourself, you can find nurturing relationships, set healthy boundaries, and re-create meaning and fulfillment in your daily life. The disconnection that you felt transforms into a feeling of being connected to the world and humanity around you. Your life unfolds like a flower. When you can release the way the past lives in you, you can create the life you want. You can show up as the person you were always meant to be.

In this book, I outline the principles that govern the family energy field, and how their violations may impact your life. You can learn to see the patterns and themes that manifest in your life and the effect of your backstory. Through simple exercises and rituals that show you how to work with your ancestral energy field energetically and easily, you can shift the burden of this field on your life.

Rituals such as these existed in almost every tradition across the globe. In this book, you will see how these have been adapted for your modern-day life so that they are not onerous or time-consuming. You do not have to be in touch with your ancestors or even know anything about your ancestors in order to do this work.

You can also identify the emotions that block you from releasing the burden of these patterns and shift them with the help of the flower essences. The essences that are needed on this healing journey and how to use them are listed in this book. Nature is there to support and heal us. Learn how the essences help your life blossom.

The book is divided into four parts.

Part I describes my own healing journey and how I learned about the family energy field and its resonance with the traditions I had been raised in. I show you how the rituals outlined in this book dovetail with my own spiritual traditions.

Part II details how to use the healing tools in the book so that they are practical and easily implemented.

Part III teaches you how violations in the family energy field show up in your life, so that you can learn to identify and start the journey of releasing them.

And finally, in Part IV, I show you how your life can blossom. Just like flowers bloom in all sorts of conditions—swamps, deserts, and sidewalks—you too can find the capacity to live life in full bloom. Honoring your roots allows you to return to connection and to yourself, lifting the unconscious, invisible barriers that keep you from finding fulfillment in your life.

PART I

# Healing My Roots

# — ONE —

# Why Heal Your Roots?

Imagine going to a party. You might feel hesitant or resistant to being there. Perhaps you were brought there by a friend. Or you might be excited to be there and the life of the party. How you carry your history within you shapes your experience of the party. Life is the party that you came to—whether you feel you were invited or not. I will show you how to carry your history within you so that you can show up as your authentic self in gratitude and appreciation for being here.

We belong to a family energy field. This field is your backstory. While a character in a novel may have only one, you have multiple backstories. However, like the readers of a novel, you don't know all of them at the start, and some, you may never know at all. Yet, whether you know them or not, these stories inhabit you. You arrive onto the stage of your life, having agreed to be in the performance, even if you don't know how the plot is going to play out.

Collectively, we carry the weight of balancing the transgenerational scales of justice, each member taking on their individual share of this burden. Fortunately, we also receive the benefit of the positive actions of our lineages, whether you are grateful or even aware of all that you have received.

Sometimes, inherited family patterns or legacies can influence your life so strongly that you may sense what you're experiencing is fate. However, it is through these patterns and legacies that your family energy field is communicating with you—in search of healing—and you can escape repeating them if you can find a way to make peace with your ancestors and progenitors.

## Can You Inherit the Fate of Your Ancestors?

Your family members, alive or departed, immediate and extended—as well as their emotions and experiences—create your family energy field. Repetition of events and their attendant emotions often serve as messengers from our family energy fields, calling us to heal the pain we carry.

Carol came to me to help her with the emotional challenges she was facing. In our sessions, she would talk about whatever she was grappling with and often shared news about her daughter, Marianna.

Now, as she sat across from me, she said, "Marianna has just been fired."

I was stunned. Carol's soft brown eyes welled up with tears, and handed her a tissue from the box on my desk.

From what I could gather, Marianna was a bold, outside-of-the-box thinker. However, her newest project at the nonprofit where she worked was controversial, Carol said, and some of Marianna's bosses and coworkers pushed back against her initiatives. "But she didn't give up, and her project is going forward!" Carol had said the last time I saw her. I could sense her pride in her daughter and the determination they both carried.

Marianna and Carol were both creative women who weren't afraid to put their ideas out there into the world and take risks professionally. Carol had headed up a department at a local hospital until her pressuring of physicians and administrators to introduce what she felt were much-needed changes led to her having been passed over for promotion. Carol had switched jobs, taking a cut in salary, because she recognized that salvaging her position would be a massive uphill battle. The stress of it all had caused her to feel very anxious and even have some panic attacks. That, in turn, had started her on a journey of healing that led her to find me.

"Do you think Marianna's situation is similar to what happened to you at the hospital? Do you feel that she pushed too hard for change, and it put people out of their comfort zone?"

Carol thought for a moment. "I didn't make that connection, but you're right. She learned that from me, I guess."

I had heard enough stories about her extended family to have spotted a pattern. Would she see it too?

"Where did you learn it from, Carol? Who in your family—your parents or grandparents—tried to change existing norms?"

Carol paused. "My father's business partners pushed him out of the business he started because they didn't want to take it in the direction he wanted to go. He was too forward-thinking for them. I guess that part of his personality got handed down to me and Marianna," she said finally.

As our conversation continued, I listened to Carol explain how her father's plans for change had been thwarted, and how his bitterness at his perceived failure colored her childhood and early years. He had carried this sadness with him to the very end until he died at a relatively young age of heart failure, or—as Carol described it—of a broken heart. Even so, his daughter and granddaughter were repeating his pattern of pressuring people too much to try to get them to change, which was causing a family pattern of suffering.

"I was just thinking about my dad the other day," Carol said. "It was his birthday, and Marianna happened to call. I could hear in her voice that she was upset. Then she broke the bad news."

*It was his birthday.* Was it a coincidence that Marianna lost her job for being too forceful about change on the birthday of her grandfather who had experienced the very same loss?

The Universe tries to get your attention in multiple ways, including through coincidences and patterns. In 1960, psychologist Carl Jung wrote in *Synchronicity: An Acausal Connecting Principle,* that synchronicity is a "meaningful coincidence of two or more events where something other than the probability of chance is involved." In other words, while they might seem to be the result of random chance, on closer examination, they have greater meaning. I've found that "mere coincidences" are worth paying attention to because they are one way the Universe can get its point across to us. Patterns of events repeating in your life or the lives of your family members are often subtle and might alert you to how your family energy fields are influencing you. These fields exist within the energy matrix human beings share with each other, the planet, and all life on earth, and they carry the memories and emotions of family members past and present.

## Seeing Patterns

When unfortunate events occur in your life, patterns can suddenly come to your attention. Along with revealing entrenched beliefs, events also shed light on emotional patterns of rejection, betrayal, and isolation that get passed down through generations. Recognizing patterns, including emotional ones, is a first step in discovering the roots of why you act, feel, and think as you do, and why the same themes and types of events keep appearing in your life even when you swear off the past. As Marianna and Carol's story shows, through repetitive patterns, you experience emotions that your ancestors might have experienced. Emotions are the connecting element between two worlds, the physical world you live in and the invisible world that you cannot see. By working with your family energy field, you can transform these patterns or family karma so that you are no longer repeating them.

Carol had never thought about the connections among three generations of her family until I brought them up. Now she could explore whether she wanted to break the pattern. While both women were determined, creative, and innovative thinkers, in her next job, Marianna might decide to try harder to pick up on the cues that she is pushing for change too hard and too fast. She might respond in a new way, one that allows her to accomplish her goals *within* an organizational structure. In working with their family pattern, Carol and Marianna's courage, determination, and creativity might become genuine assets, leading to fulfilling positions as well as meaningful change in their workplaces.

Ancestral energy patterns come in many forms and play out in different ways. For instance, behavioral patterns may be easily visible. As much as you don't like to admit this, your behaviors do mirror those of your parents and generations prior. Some of us are frugal, others get angry quickly, a few are overly suspicious. You may also have patterns of being generous or feeling passionate about issues. Sometimes, themes remain the same in relationship after relationship. And in families, the themes reappear several generations in a row. A "family curse" is real: it's a repetition of an old energetic pattern passed down the family tree. Maybe you have known someone who vowed they would never again get involved with a certain type of romantic partner. Then you saw that, despite their falling for someone who on the surface was very different from their previous partner, the same old dynamic was at play in this person's new relationship. Maybe you have experienced this yourself. You might say you will never again become involved with someone who is hypercritical only to end up with a partner who doesn't openly criticize you but shows you through their actions that they disapprove of you. Or maybe you're in a relationship with someone who respects and supports you but complains that you're very critical of them. It's as if you're in the same relationship you were before, only with the roles reversed.

There is another kind of pattern that I call "experiential patterns." These are instances where you see the same kinds of experiences recurring across generations. A grandfather was betrayed by his business partner, and the same type of thing happens again to his son and to his grandson. Or someone faces constant setbacks in their professional pursuits, and this pattern repeats itself. While it's possible to call this a "family curse," if there are positive patterns, you call them "family blessings." Or more broadly, you may even call this "family karma."

Many of us accept these patterns as karmic—something you have to accept and live with. But what if there is more to this than meets the eye? What if there is a message behind these patterns? I call this *what is it that is wanting to be seen*. What if you need to unlock something to release yourself and also those who may come after you from repeating these patterns?

As decades of research on the psychology of emotion has shown, each of us has a response system that is activated by a range of triggers. What if your emotional response system is a window into understanding some of these patterns you are trapped in? And what if, by developing an understanding of this system and these underlying family patterns, you can then start to unlock the cycles of behavior and experiences you may have found yourself in? Does your frugality come from honoring the earth or due to a fear of lack? Does your worry about not having enough manifest in you holding yourself back and not taking some risk, thus putting a ceiling on your professional life? Or does this emotion and behavior make its presence felt by having too many possessions that clutter your home (hoarding), or by your demanding financial control of your partner? Do you feel that *you* are not enough? Who else in your family has felt this way? What is the origin of this story you tell yourself? I encourage you to begin to journal some of the answers to these questions, but you will also explore them more deeply in later chapters.

If you stop to notice how your family energy field influences your life, you can be more conscious of any decisions you make in that moment of choice. Will you do what you've always tended to do, or will you pivot, breaking out of an old pattern of action and reaction?

My own experience has shown me that letting go of old habits and establishing new ones can be very difficult. If you don't consciously choose a new way of thinking, feeling, or acting, your unconscious chooses the familiar path. When I started noticing and working with patterns, I wasn't aware that I resisted making plans far out into the future. Planning vacations or social events too far ahead of time was fraught with anxiety for me. My parents didn't like to plan too far ahead either, perhaps because of my father's unpredictable travel schedule, but as an adult with my own children, I didn't have to deal with this when making plans. My unease about looking at hotel websites to compare and contrast lodgings made no sense. It took me a long while to realize that I was repeating an old family pattern.

In working with clients, I notice that knowledge of patterns, while important, very often isn't enough to lead to significant personal transformation. Someone might be fiercely determined to leave behind old habits and work hard to change them only to find themselves in the grip of their family patterns again and again. When they make a choice, they may fall back into their old ways—often, without realizing it. If they're conscious of being at a fork in the road, able to step out in a new direction, they can find themselves unconsciously resisting the change they vowed to make and moving back to familiar territory. Or they procrastinate. Or they make a mistake and accidentally sabotage themselves. They deny the truth that's obvious to people around them who aren't caught in the pattern: that they are once again putting themselves in the same position they were in before.

## Filling the Void

Behind these patterns are emotions. I see emotions as a transmitting signal that each of us unconsciously sends out. This phenomenon was studied by neuroscientist Candace Pert, Ph.D., and formed the thesis of her groundbreaking book, *Molecules of Emotion*. In an interview with SixSeconds.org, she describes this process: "As our feelings change, this mixture of peptides travels throughout your body and your brain. And they're literally changing the chemistry of every cell in your body—and sending out vibrations to other people. We're not just little hunks of meat. We're vibrating like a tuning fork—we send out a vibration to other people. We broadcast and receive. Thus the emotions orchestrate the interactions among all our organs and systems to control that. You have receptors on every cell in your body. They actually are little mini electrical pumps. So we're actually sending out various electrical signals—vibrations. We're all familiar with one kind of vibration: When we talk, we send a vibration through the air that someone else perceives as sound... You are connected to everybody else. Your emotions are key. And you are leaving a wake, changing the world around you in a huge way."

Humans have been governed by the same emotions for thousands of years even though our lives have grown more complex with changes in ecology, technology, information overload, and shifting lifestyles. You might connect and identify with these emotions whether they happen in history books, sci-fi fantasies, news stories, or even animated films. You might even function within a narrow emotional range—anxious, overwhelmed, tired, impatient, quick to anger, critical of others and yourself, or easily taking offense. Your emotional signals might be verbal or expressed through your behavior. When you are constantly in the grip of these emotions, they can cause you to weep, overeat, break out in road rage, and feel overwhelmed and stressed. You might even hope that people will receive your messages and respond to your unconscious distress signals: "I'm angry and you don't understand what I'm going through" or "I'm hurting, and I need help."

Negative emotions can be seen as messengers of your hidden needs and therefore have value. You can even view your sadness and your despair as an invitation to a deeper exploration of your hidden connection to a higher consciousness. When you're at the end of your rope, in despair, you may turn to the spiritual world for hope and relief. Your emotions can then be seen as a gateway to building faith and spiritual connection—an invisible, unseen realm. Emotions like contentment, acceptance, compassion, and enthusiasm, on the other hand, may be less frequent, buried under the demands of your life and relationships. But these are the emotions that can make you sing, dance, smile, love, reach out to others, and take risks.

You may want to expand your emotional range so that you are not always circling in the same range of negative emotions like frustration, sadness, anger, powerlessness, or despair. But how do you expand your emotional range, and perhaps even operate more consistently from a different emotional frequency?

In his book *Flourish*, Martin Seligman, Ph.D., talks about how in his thirty-five-year practice as a psychotherapist, he saw that helping his patients rid themselves of their anxiety, sadness, and anger did not result in happy patients. Instead, he got "empty patients." The absence of negative emotions does not guarantee happiness. He points out that experiencing positive emotions is a sign of positive mental health. The skills for becoming happy are completely different from the skills for not being anxious, sad, or angry.

Working with energetic healers over the years, I have become aware that when you take out negative emotions, you need to replace them with positive emotions. How do you fill the void left by negative emotions you have released? One way to do this is through the power of flowers!

For centuries, flowers have tugged at our hearts. You may offer them as symbols of your love, your grief, your devotion, and in celebration. You might buy them when you need to uplift yourself. They speak more eloquently than words with their color, their smell, their delicate petals, their impermanence, and their quiet movement to fullness. They are a universal and time-less symbol of the heart. To imagine a world without flowers is to see a world without love and beauty.

More than its beauty, each flower has a positive emotional resonance that is a function of where it grows, how it spreads its seeds, its color, and the structure of its leaves and stems. Flowers carry the life force of the plant—the force through which pol-lination and reproduction of the species happen—and are the glorious, colorful, and most creative way in which the plant expresses itself.

Flower essences—the energetic imprint of the flower in water—lift and transform thought patterns and their associated emotions by shifting negative judgments, creating calmness and clarity, and allowing us to see an issue differently. For instance, willow flower essence can shift and transform bitterness into forgiveness and gratitude. Mimulus helps people who are shy by opening the door to a feeling of courage. Mustard, like the golden yellow flowers, can lift the blues when they descend on you sud-denly and your spirits feel low. Flower essences work through an awareness of polarity. For instance, while taking them, you might become aware that you are depressed, but also of an uplifting of your spirit. In this way, there is a transformation that occurs through an awareness of the polarities of your emotions.

As Dr. Bach, credited with rediscovering and develop-ing a system of flower essences, said in "Some Fundamental Considerations of Disease," published in *Homeopathic World*, 1930, when you get rid of negative emotions, "an adverse force has gone, but a space exists where it has been situated." There is a void that needs to be filled. Essences help us fill it.

A healing insight needs to be integrated into a new per-spective of seeing your world. It is a journey from victimhood, anger, fear, and loss to hope, compassion, faith, and empower-ment. This is where I see flower essences can help create and sustain transformation.

When my own resistances step in, and I'm aware of what I'm doing and why I'm reacting a particular way, I lean on the flower essences. For instance, as it relates to my anxiety in relation to making travel arrangements, with the help of flower essences, I don't have to let my unconscious and the old family pattern interfere and stop me from making travel plans early.

I am not a trained therapist or psychologist. However, I believe that my training as an economist and many years of aca-demic research taught me to search for an answer to my "why?" Why do people feel this way? Why do these patterns appear? Economists often examine how people and institutions respond or fail to respond to incentives. That's what I did too! I stud-ied emotions and became a certified flower essence practitioner. Having studied emotions and how they express themselves, I wanted to see what was driving the emotions I was observing. Without my realizing it, I was being led to a study of family as an energy field and how disturbances in this energy field mani-fested in our lives. I began an advanced study in family constel-lation therapy—an approach that examines how emotions are connected to the family energy field.

When a client comes to me, I'm listening and feeling between the lines for the emotions they are expressing—or not express-ing. I notice the direction their emotions are taking me, what I'm starting to think about or feel while listening to them, and what I'm starting to identify as not just a casual remark or observa-tion of theirs but something significant. As I interact with the client, I try to identify these emotions and see where they came from. Did they originate in the family field? How do they keep expressing themselves in my client's life? Is there one key issue they are dealing with that they might not even be aware of?

Based on my observations, I select a custom blend of flower essences. Although at first, I don't necessarily know how these emotions might go back to their parents, their grandparents, or even further, I start searching for patterns that might repeat in their relationships, in events, in their families. I search for an emotional pattern that may be related to a family pattern to help them shift their energy. Sometimes, I may hear someone say, "We're not emotionally expressive. We don't talk about problems; we behave as if everything is fine." That response, especially to a loss or a betrayal, can suppress important emotions of anger, sadness, or grief. They might fear experiencing the depth of their anger or grief and feel ashamed that they aren't simply "getting over" the loss and moving on as they think they should. These emotional patterns can powerfully affect us, but there is a way to shift them through flower essences. They can help create new ways of feeling and behaving. Throughout this book, I'll offer some suggested flower essence combinations that I have used with clients so that you can begin trying this form of energy medicine.

Through family constellation therapy, I discovered the challenge we all face is honoring our family energy field while honoring ourselves. Through this journey, I was led back to my roots in ways I would never have expected.

## What Happens When Your Ancestors Fail to Move On?

One afternoon during a holiday to Iceland a few years ago, I was riding in a car through the countryside. I closed my eyes for a moment and suddenly felt a huge crowd around me. Startled, I opened my eyes, but only quiet fields and open meadows were outside the car window. When I leaned back and closed my eyes again, I felt the same thronging crowds. I became aware that they were wearing old-fashioned clothes. When I opened my eyes, nothing! I didn't know what was happening. I later learned about seeing beyond this physical reality to become aware of souls that are earthbound.

I was seeing ancestors that day on the road in Iceland. Whose were they? I don't know. What if you are surrounded by your ancestors, just like the crowd I sensed during my car ride?

Your physical features, your health or ill health, your talents, and many of your beliefs can be linked to your parents, grandparents, and probably to your ancestors. Indian spiritual teachers believe there are also strong blood karmic ties not just between previous and current generations, but also future unborn generations. Indian astrological charts also show traits and patterns that are shared between the grandchild and grandparent. How does this connection express itself? You might think you are acting independently of your past, but it shows up in your life anyway.

It's almost as if the dead remain attached to their family in the physical world. Indian spiritual teachers might say that their souls roam unsatisfied, unfinished with their worldly desires, craving a taste for the material world. In India, the Sanskrit word *maya* is often loosely translated as attachment to the material world and the illusion that life is nothing greater than these attachments. Yet, the ultimate journey of the soul is beyond these illusions, toward freedom from attachments and into enlightenment.

So, just like us, your ancestors, or at least some of them, can be trapped by their desires and attachments in the field of illusion

instead of a movement toward enlightenment. In my Indian traditions, a key part of ancestral rituals are prayers for the souls of our
ancestors. It is believed that our ancestors going back seven generations influence us and can impact seven generations to come.
Many Native American traditions, such as those of the Iroquois,
believe this too. The basis of this ritual is gratitude—for your life
on this earth and for what you have received from your ancestors. How many generations of ancestors can you recall? If you
counted all of your ancestors going back seven generations, you'd
have two hundred and fifty-four mothers and fathers responsible
for you being here today—all who would be in your family energy
field—the details of whose lives and names are lost to time. If you
go back twenty generations, you have one million ancestors!

In fact, many Indian teachers argue that most souls are not
able to transit out of the earth plane and are restless and stag-
nant, unable to ascend to a more peaceful realm. Buddhism
also acknowledges the existence of a realm that is populated
by suffering souls. The term *earthbound*, an expression in older
English writings, is also used to refer to the spirit of a family
member that did not move out of the earth plane. Clearly different traditions point to varying levels of awareness among
those who have passed on. In India, you even have rituals to
clear the land and space before starting construction or moving
into a new home or office. These ceremonies help the healing
of the earth and those souls who may still be connected to that
physical space.

When you work with your family energy field, you heal your
roots. You release the unconscious patterns that act as a ceiling on your life, on your potential, and on your happiness. As
you heal your roots, your life can blossom. If your family has
been a source of pain or trauma in your life or if your recently

deceased ancestors were abusive or dysfunctional, it's hard to imagine wanting to honor them. But you certainly don't want their energies hanging around. Paradoxically, the act of honoring family keeps them from doing additional damage to your life. When you reject or disrespect them out of fear or anger, you never resolve the unconscious patterns of poverty, violence, depression, and unhappiness. And it's not just you, but also your ancestors who stay stuck. When you heal your roots, you release the family patterns that hold you back.

## What to Expect in This Book: The Journey Ahead

In this book, I will give you a glimpse into an invisible world. I introduce you to your family energy field, how it affects you and manifests in your life. I will show you how to work with this field energetically while building your relationship with yourself. I will teach you how to do this with the help of flower essences and traditions adapted from my Indian heritage.

In the next few chapters, I describe my own journey into healing my roots and understanding the significance of the traditions I was raised in. In Part II, I show you how you can use flower essences—a form of energy medicine—and rituals adapted from my traditions to heal your roots. These are simple tools that you can use. Understanding the transgenerational burden you carry and how it affects you is discussed in Part III. It includes the principles that govern the family energy field and shape your backstory. In this section, I provide exercises that help you shift or release the unconscious burden of these stories. And finally, in Part IV, I offer suggestions that will help your life blossom. Ultimately, you need to honor yourself as well as your lineage in order to receive love and find self-worth. It's important that you not lose yourself in this journey to connect with your roots or your lineage, but rather find yourself through the process.

While you read this book, I recommend that you keep a journal to record what you discover about your own personal transgenerational patterns as they come to your awareness. This way, you can start to see the stories that have shaped you and begin to note down your own thoughts about the path you have taken. You might also begin researching and collecting the items and information that will help you build your own ancestral altars and create your own prayers in order to heal your family energy fields that I discuss in Part II. You may feel that you do not have this information or access to this information. Don't worry. Once you start looking for details about relatives and forebearers, information may come unexpectedly, as I discovered. For me and my clients, material came in the form of photographs, phone calls, and in other unexpected ways. However, you also do not need to know your ancestors at all to do the work in this book—if you were adopted, for example.

I also recommend that you take note of your emotions as you journal your reactions in the next few weeks. I always recommend journaling to my clients who take flower essences. When you do that, it brings awareness to the shifts that are taking place. You can even choose a journal that is half blank at the top and half ruled at the bottom. This kind of format allows you to write as well as draw or add images that lend themselves to this process such as maps, a family tree, or anything else that comes up. You can keep colored pencils or paint handy that you can use in this portion. I would recommend buying a new journal for this purpose, even if it is just a plain black book. Although it need not be expensive, you might also want to try to look for one that appeals to you on some level.

To get you started, I have listed two exercises below.

## Journal Exercises

1. How to Start Working with Your Lineage

   Do you see patterns of experiences or events that run in your family? Perhaps some of these are obvious to you. You might have always noticed them, thought little of them, or treated them simply as a coincidence. Are there particular ages when patterns repeat? You might wish to start with your nuclear family and then move up the maternal or paternal line. Pick just one side of your family to start with. Are there behaviors or emotions that seem to underlie these events or experiences that are similar? There can be one predominant emotion or multiple emotions. Make a note of them. You will return to these in the next few chapters.

2. Stories Play Out in Many Ways

   As you think about your family story, try this exercise. Write down your family's story, starting with the words, "In my family, we . . ." This isn't about morality and ideals but about what you and your family members typically experience. It's a way for you to see the patterns that might run through your family. For example:

   > "In our family, we give too much to others at great expense to ourselves, and no one ever seems to appreciate that."

   > "In our family, marriages never seem to last. The men are always betraying the women."

If you have trouble identifying your family story, think of some of the sayings and tales your family tells over and over again. What's the takeaway of each story? Do you see a common thread of how you "always" seem to have some experiences and "never" seem to have others?

You might add some detail about why you and your relatives believe your family has certain patterns of experience.

Next, write down some examples of how that story is true for you and your family. How has the story played out? Think about yourself, your siblings, your parents, and your grandparents. Then think about your cousins, aunts and uncles, and more distant relatives. Now try to think of some examples of how the family story isn't true. Who did something different and broke the pattern? Was it hard for that person to change your family's "karma" and experience something different? How did the family respond to this relative breaking the family pattern?

Go back to looking at your family story as you wrote it. How does it make you feel? Does it make you sad? Frustrated? Proud? Helpless? Then think about any example or examples of a relative trying to break the pattern that you identified. How do you feel about what happened when that family member rebelled against the story? What, if anything, does this tell you about your family story and its power? See if you can identify the emotional, behavioral, and experiential patterns that run in your family.

# TWO

# The Power of
# the Unseen

As I look back, maybe I never really came to learn economics. Perhaps the seeds of my journey had been planted long
ago. My father was a man of few words, but he loved to tell stories. I had heard one in particular about the merchant of Basra
many times. I have since discovered this story, as my father
told it, was based on the one by W. Somerset Maugham called
"Appointment at Samarra." It was one of his favorites, I think,
because my father had a keen appreciation for the inevitability
of fate. Here is how that story goes:

Abu Bakr is strolling in the marketplace in Baghdad when
he sees the God of Death. Frightened, he takes his best steed and
flees to Basra. There, he meets the God of Death again.

"What are you doing here, my lord?' he asks. "I saw you in
Baghdad and came to Basra to flee you!"

"Yes," the God of Death replied. "I was surprised to see you in
Baghdad because I knew I had to meet you here in Basra today."

Maybe, like Abu Bakr, I had to travel to America to learn
flower essences—a type of energy medicine—for healing emotions. Had someone told me back in college that I would someday

study and teach people about their family karma, I would have laughed off the idea. Beliefs about fate—or karma as we call it in India—and how to heal it? *Those were for people who weren't educated and sophisticated* was the message that I had received in many ways over many years.

In the end, my journey took me back to a place that had nurtured and nourished me, India—a place that had always lived inside of me, my spiritual home. I came to understand that my destiny was a combination of my fate—the family of origin that I was born into, my country, my education—and the choices I have made since. I came to realize that while fate is inevitable, we have the power of choice within us to respond to it so we can create our own destiny.

Destiny is the master plan of our soul that we come to manifest, invisible to us, but making its presence felt in every twist and turn of fate. Destiny is our invisible partnership with the Universe. In India, we were taught as children to acknowledge, if not to be in partnership with, the Universe.

When I was growing up, faith was part of the daily fabric of our life—in the marigold garlands heaped untidily under the peepul tree, in the colorful, sometimes garish pictures of gods and goddesses that hung from the rearview mirrors of the noisy auto-rickshaws and fancy cars. It was in the smell of incense as vendors opened their stores after morning prayers. And it was in the sound of the call of the muezzin in the morning, the temple bells in the evening, or the songs of the itinerant singer on the weekend. It was hard to escape the presence of faith and yet, so pervasive to be almost invisible. It hung over the air in everything that was said or done.

People around us were constantly fasting. It wasn't just Meatless Monday—it could be any day of the week, depending on whom you were worshipping. Long lines snaked around the temple to Hanuman on Tuesday, around the Saint Shirdi Sai's temple on Thursday, and there were invocations to the Goddess on Friday. Little ragged beggar children held tin cans with mustard oil at the traffic lights on Saturday. If I wished, I could see my reflection and drop a coin in for Sani, the destructive planet and great teacher. If faith was pervasive, then miracles were proof of the Divine. They had to go together.

One day our doorbell rang. Our little patch of green with its white railings and terracotta pots bordered a large covered white marble veranda that offered shade in the sweltering heat of the Indian summer. On the other side, our driveway led down to black iron gates. Visitors didn't just lift the latch, swing open the gate, walk up the driveway, cross the cool veranda, and bang on the door with the imposing brass knockers. No, they would wait outside the iron gates after ringing the bell there. Someone from the household would then come out to the balcony upstairs and look down to see who it could be, to gauge whether or not the visitor was worth the trek down a flight of stairs to open the large teak doors that allowed entrance to the house.

It was my mother who peered out. A sadhu, a wandering seeker, stood at the gate. His hair was unkempt, matted and coarse, and twisted into medium strands. He was naked to the waist, a loincloth around him, a wooden staff, a small brass pot or *kamandal*, signifying his status in the world. Bereft of material possessions, he was dependent on the mercy of strangers for food.

"Mother, I'm hungry and thirsty," he called up to her. "I need some food. I've been walking for days."

"Okay, Baba. Wait, and I'll send something down." *Baba* is a term of respect used to denote an older man.

The old man squatted near the gate to wait. "You can come inside and sit in the shade if you like," said my mother, heading back inside.

"Bindu," she called to our help, "give him a cup of tea, some *atta* to make his *rotis*, and some vegetables." *Atta* is whole wheat flour used to make rotis, or unleavened circular bread similar to tortillas.

I still stood at the railing, watching, listening, and learning, as a child does. Bedraggled as he was, he was not worthy of dismissal. A mendicant at our door in need of food would never be turned away. It was an unwritten code, not just in our house but probably in innumerable houses all over India, at least before the advent of twenty-four-hour television and multistoried apartments.

As Bindu went downstairs, my mother came back again and watched with me from the balcony. The sadhu put his hand out for the tea and looked at the bag of atta in Bindu's hand that she held out. He looked up at my mother.

"I cannot cook this. I do not stop anywhere. Will you give me something I can eat?" he asked. His tone was not pleading, but matter of fact. He was on his way to the foothills of the Himalayas.

"Then it will take a little time. Is that okay?"

It was afternoon, not yet time for dinner, but lunch was definitely over. My mother and Bindu went to work in the kitchen and made some rotis. The ones that they made were thick—designed to fill you up, not the thin, fluffy kind that my father would eat. My mother scooped handfuls of vegetables into the rotis and took them down on a stainless-steel plate, or *thali*. The old man accepted it gratefully from her, sat down on his haunches, and, with the food before him, bent his head to eat his meal. My mother went and stood to the side. When he finished, he rinsed his hands and called out to her.

"Come here," he said. "You have been very kind to me. I will give you something. Hold my hair in your fingers and think of what you want."

"That's all right, Baba," my mother said. "I don't want anything."

"No! Hold my hair."

Gingerly, my mother held a coiled strand of his matted hair between her index finger and her thumb. A steady stream of water started to flow from his hair onto the ground. My mother started to laugh.

"Don't laugh," he reprimanded her. "Your wish will be fulfilled. Now, do you have any money?"

"Yes, I do. I have five hundred rupees," said my mother trustingly, thinking of the money my father had left to pay for the repair of the countertop in the kitchen.

"Will you be sorry if you lose it?" said the old man.

"No, I won't."

"Very well, then. Bring it!"

My mother went and brought the five hundred rupees that my father had left and handed it to him. He took it between his fingers and as he rubbed it, he muttered some words, and right before my mother's eyes, it turned to ash. He scattered it over the driveway and garden and then from a small bag he fished out a few grains of dried wheat. He gave these to my mother.

"Whatever you are wishing for will be fulfilled." And with that, he raised his hand in blessing, turned, and walked away.

When my father came home, we told him the story. Although those five hundred rupees were a significant sum for both of them, he heard the story and accepted it as one of the unusual, yet acceptable occurrences of daily life in India. My mother says she still has the grains of wheat that the mendicant gave her. She keeps them on her altar, and the story still makes her laugh. Although she didn't share what she wished for, she said it did come true.

Incidents like this opened up our minds to what we would normally consider impossible. Faith can arrive as a beggar at your gate. As you journey up the spiritual path, it is possible to manifest these "miracles." However, for the true mystic, these are considered distractions from the ultimate goal of experiencing that constant unity of consciousness.

Despite being of the same religion, my parents practiced it in different ways. My mother veered toward the mystical, spiritual aspect of her faith and seldom went to the temple, whereas my father was more likely to turn to a more traditional form of religion. I remember once when my father had a problem at work, he went to the little roadside temple each week with an offering of *boondi*—delicious tiny yellow balls clustered together with the syrup they had been soaked in. His faith had an element of hope and surrender. Often, my sister or I would go with my father. Little children lined up outside the temple, and we distributed the sweet little yellow balls among their eager, grubby fingers while my mother did her evening prayers at home.

Across India, a multiplicity of faiths, traditions, and religious outlooks meet within a household so that different members might practice in different ways or even worship different deities depending on what they were drawn to. I went to a Catholic school, and often my friends and I got off the bus, went through the open doors of the church, and then out to school. It didn't seem to matter to us that none of us were Catholic.

Different ways of practicing faith, leading to the same hope that problems were in the hands of the Spirit, to be sorted out in the best possible way and in divine time.

## The Dispensation of Hope

Faith was a way of coping with the inevitability of fate, the uncertainty of outcomes, and the stress of it all. Faith dispensed hope, but growing up, astrologers were also the dispensers of hope.

When my son was born here in the US, my gynecologist sent me a token that heralded the moment of his birth. I looked at the small porcelain shoe in my hand, the delicate lettering wrapped around the entire shoe, proclaiming my son's name, his height, weight, and date and time of birth. Soft baby blue ribbon, reserved for boys, was woven into the shoe where the laces would be. I was delighted with it, though I marveled at the way the most private of information, the time of his arrival on earth, could now be under the gaze of the public eye.

In India, that information was private. If you knew the time and date of your birth, you could give it to any astrologer, who could now tell you about your personality, your family life, your character, temperament, the state of your finances, and even hints of your past life. Long before you could put this information into a computer that would spit out pages of esoteric perfect squares inlaid with triangles, the astrologer would painstakingly calculate your original birth chart and the current position of the planets. Knowledge was handed from father to son; it was a tedious and long series of calculations. In times of trouble, you made an appointment with your family astrologer—an important name in your little black book. Their consultation never had a price. Their payment was whatever you chose.

I remember the astrologers who would visit my grandmother's or my parents' homes. Sometimes friends or relatives would send them to us as well. They would be respectfully welcomed and hospitably served. My mother, depending on the ebb and flow of our family life, would be interested or uninterested in what they had to say. My father would treat them with respect but distance himself from the conversation, leaving it to my mother to inquire on his behalf. I wasn't sure how much he ever believed in them. Yet, the family horoscopes were kept carefully wrapped in red fabric and opened only after we had bathed and when the astrologer came. It was a ceremonial affair.

My sister and I could barely contain our excitement as we grew older and understood what these visits were about. When the day would come, we would dress carefully in cotton tunics and leggings with the traditional long scarf thrown over our shoulders in a semblance of modesty, hoping that perhaps ours would be read this time. Given the time and effort to do those calculations by hand, only one or two horoscopes would be read in a day, and we never knew whose turn it would be, especially since sometimes an aunt, uncle, or an older cousin might come who would have precedence over us. *Panditji*, as they were called, would usually be dressed in a white collarless shirt and a fine white muslin dhoti wrapped around his waist and legs like a loose pant, giving him plenty of room to sit comfortably on a floor cross-legged. The red mark on his forehead indicated that he had showered, shaved, and finished his morning prayers and meditation—nothing would be done without the grace and blessing of the Goddess.

Although I still do not fully understand astrology, I began to believe that in a well-ordered Universe, our birth could not be a random event: it was a precise outcome, with the planets and stars aligned for this journey. However, I also saw that we live through hope—we must believe in self-determination on some level in order to carry on life. After much contemplation, I realized that while fate was inevitable, this is how hope was dispensed: Panditji would always give you things to do. Sometimes they asked you to feed the birds, the cows, the indigent, almost always recite some prayers—you never came away with nothing to do. Although you may never do what he asked you to do—it depended on how easy it was to accomplish it—you came away being asked to connect with the Divine or the Universe and to surrender your problems to a higher power through often simple acts of charity and prayer.

My mother's family was academic, westernized, outspoken in their ideas and views of the world. Many of my cousins and relatives were atheists. My father's family, on the other hand, was traditional, conservative, and religious. My mother, like a trapeze artist, would swing between these two worlds—more spiritual than religious, and more mystical than ritualistic. I was scooped up in the mystery of it all, growing up between this polarity.

## The Arrival of Haripriya

My parents kept an open house, and we had a constant stream of visitors and long-term guests while I was growing up. We had guests who would stay for months, having come for medical treatment, to go to college, or find a house and a job. With this heady cocktail of visitors, lunch and dinner could end up being lengthy, animated affairs with wide-ranging discussions about everything under the sun. Hot, languid Indian summer evenings were spent playing in the park outside our house with the neighborhood kids.

One day, we came home to find a new woman at our house. She wore pale saffron robes and spoke with a heavy European accent. Her chador or shawl was pulled tightly around her shoulders and around her neck was her *rudraksha mala*, her prayer beads.

"This is Haripriya," my mother said. "She will stay with us for a while."

We tried not to stare, but my sister and I had never seen anyone like her. Haripriya was sick and needed a place to recover. She came into our lives and remained a seasonal fixture for the next few decades. She was affectionate and talked endlessly. She was very warm and inviting, and yet she had no problem disciplining my sister and me, and she did so often. It was unthinkable for us to argue back.

Haripriya, or Anne—which was her name although we never called her that—stayed for months in India, avoiding the fall and deepening winter in Switzerland. During that time, she would shuttle between Delhi, Calcutta (now Kolkata), and her little cottage in the Kalyanvan ashram in the foothills of the Himalayas. With the arrival of the summer heat in India, she would go back to Switzerland to work as a nurse for the terminally ill.

Haripriya was strong. Her hands were thick and capable, her hair was cut short, and her words had a little clip to them. When her words sometimes failed her, she would use sounds to express herself. Mostly, she spoke English with a smattering of Bengali words thrown in that no one but my mother understood. At the start of her visit with us, she was always very particular about her *thali* (the traditional metal plate in which food was served) from which she ate, and the glass from which she drank water. But as the weeks wore on, she slipped into the routine of the household that was part and parcel of our lives. She, like everyone else who came and stayed at our home for months on end, was always welcome and no one was ever expected to pay for rent or food: that was unthinkable. If needed, my mother would even give her own food to an unexpected lunch or dinner guest. No one went hungry. This was just how my mother had been raised.

As Haripriya told it, she had been watching television one day in Switzerland when they showed a documentary about Anandamayi Ma, an Indian spiritual teacher and yoga guru. "At that moment, I got up and said, 'I'm going to India to find her.'" And so, along with a friend, she drove across Iran, Afghanistan, Pakistan, and into India in a Jeep.

"There was a cloud of dust, and the Afghan horsemen came galloping," she said and made the sound of hooves clattering with rhythmic, clipped syllables. "They wanted to take us somewhere, but I took out my cigarettes and gave each of them one and lit it," she said, making the flicking motion of a lighter with her hand. "They were very appreciative and polite, and they let us go."

Haripriya's road trip was full of adventure, and her stories enthralled my sister and me. After arriving in India, she searched Anandamayi Ma out and never went back to her old lifestyle. We, of course, had never heard of Ma, so Haripriya took my mother, my sister, and me to see her. As a little girl, I remember the crowds towering over me and barely being able to see Ma on a stage in the front. I mostly recall feeling frustrated by the heat and the mosquitoes.

It was Haripriya who regaled us with stories of Ma's miracles and gave me the book *Autobiography of a Yogi* when I was twelve. The book was not about Anandamayi Ma, but one of her contemporaries, Paramhansa Yogananda, and it described a magical meeting between the two of them. The spark was lit. In India, we are open to finding an enlightened master because we know that such teachers can be the hollow flute through which divine music is heard. After reading *Autobiography of a Yogi*, all about an Indian monk and yogi's quest for his spiritual teacher, I too launched into a determined quest for an enlightened master. As a young girl, I wanted to experience what he had felt when he met his teacher—a window into the portal of divinity. In the years that followed (in addition to my interest in contraband Levi jeans and the latest fashions), I searched incessantly for mystical India. I wanted to find my own teacher—a guide to help focus my faith, the way Ma had done for Haripriya.

I was in my late teens when I heard of an enlightened monk through a stranger that came to my parents' house to drop off a package. My interest was piqued, and I was determined to meet him. A few years later, I discovered that he would be near Delhi where I lived, and I finally had a chance to meet him. I remember reaching the ashram and being told to wait in the foyer. Suddenly, the door opened and the teacher I had been searching for came out. In that instant, I felt I was surrounded by love I had never experienced anything like it before!

"I've been waiting for you," he said as he held his arms out. I forgot to touch his feet, as was the custom in my culture, and hugged him. Later on, I came to realize that the cocooning, uplifting, and protective love I experienced in that moment with such certainty and deep knowing was divine, unconditional love.

After I found my teacher, I also encouraged my sister to meet him, and she too felt the same connection. We both began to follow him, although our parents did not. My father said his family didn't follow any gurus, and my mother, although more open perhaps because of the arrival of Haripriya, said that she did not feel drawn to him as her teacher. However, neither of them stopped my sister and me from visiting him. In fact, our teacher would sometimes communicate to us through my mother. As my mother sat in meditation, she would tell my sister or me, "Swamiji is in Delhi. Call him!" We would call the ashram and immediately be told to come over. Other times, my mother would have an inkling that he was there, and sure enough, the phone would ring.

"*Behn*! Where are my two daughters?" *Behn* means "sister" in Hindi.

"Swamiji, I'm sending them," she would say. My mother told us that we were so scattered that Swamiji had to communicate through her. Whenever Swamiji reached out, my mother would bustle us off to the ashram to spend time with our teacher.

Because my family lived and breathed faith as part of our everyday life, as a child I was unaware of what a privilege it was to be around Swamiji, and to be given his time, love, and attention. Swamiji would often reproach my mother for having made us too westernized. Perhaps we were. For instance, sometimes our teacher would give us some food from his thali. We didn't want to eat it due to western influences, but my mother would tell us later that a guru's food was consecrated.

Born and raised on the axis of colonialism, I believed I had been given an excellent education in India in the Catholic school and later, the competitive Jesuit institution I had attended. However, the philosophies of Indian spiritual and religious traditions were never part of the curriculum. Later, I was to learn that my education was part of a deliberate policy. India was a part of Imperial Britain. Almost two hundred years ago, a British nobleman, Lord Thomas Babington Macaulay, had sailed to the south of India to meet the Governor-General, the representative of the British crown in India. In his *Minute on Education* (1835) deeply impressed by the achievements of Western civilization, he wrote of his opinion that English should be made the court language of India, that the British should "do our best to form a class of persons, Indian in blood and color and English in taste, opinions, in morals and in intellect." Although India successfully fought for its independence from Britain, Macaulay had left his mark on Indian culture. Two centuries later, I had felt that the best way to use my talents had to involve Western knowledge and university degrees. It would be many years before I would begin to question the ideas that had taken root in my home country and explore a perspective that many of my peers dismissed.

## Leaving India

Growing up in India, poverty was everywhere. For as long as I can remember, I wanted to do something to change it. Sometimes, the persistent poverty desensitized us to its presence, but there was no escaping it. Somehow, I thought that this road to change would start with economics so that is what I studied as an undergraduate in India and went on to study in England for my master's degree. I returned to India, excited to put my skills to the test, and joined a private policy think tank. It didn't take long to realize that the journey from the bottom to the top of the professional totem pole was going to be a long one for me. Everyone who had a say about anything had a doctorate, and so I considered going back to England to pursue one myself. My warm-hearted, gregarious boss, who had a doctorate from an Ivy League university in the US, would tell me repeatedly, "Anu, you have to get your Ph.D., and America's the place to go—it's the land of milk and honey! Forget about England." He was passionate, but I was less than enthusiastic. However, fate was to intervene in the form of two letters.

The first was from the University of Cambridge in England telling me that since I had gone back to India for a year after my master's degree, I was no longer eligible for any financial aid for the doctorate, an important detail that would influence my choices. The second letter came a few months later from a university in Rhode Island offering me admission and financial aid. Where was Rhode Island? Was it really an island? I didn't know, and in any case, I didn't really care because I didn't want to go. America was so far away from my family and my home, and I didn't know anyone in Rhode Island.

After my unwelcome letter from Cambridge, I had shed copious tears. My mother told me to pull myself together and consider going to the United States to get a doctorate. I couldn't go back to England, and if I was going to really do something, I felt that I needed the credentials. My mother, though recognizing that America was far away, encouraged me. Her eldest sister had left their small town in Assam and traveled by boat to study in Calcutta. At that time, on the eve of India's independence, it was a two-day journey by train and ferry.

My grandfather had never even left Assam. Yet in just two generations, my mother's brothers had gone on to study overseas, traveling by ship to London and Italy. So, although she might have had reservations, it was not beyond the realm of possibility. But I wanted to stay close. I had loved the independence of England, but I had missed my family. Now, the time for a decision was drawing close. I had to get a visa, reply to the university in the US, and make preparations to leave. I felt sick to my stomach. Somehow, something miraculous would need to happen if I was not going to go to the United States. But so far nothing had, so here I was, between what I saw as a rock and a hard place.

One afternoon close to the deadline, I went and stood next to my father without looking at him. The rain had stopped. The smell of wet earth mingled with the rain and the air was somewhat cool. My father stood on the balcony and looked out at the park in front of our house. I looked out too. The grass was tall from the monsoon rains. Rose-ringed parakeets swooped down and then up over the rooftops. I wanted to ask him what he thought. I found a point in the park that I could fix my gaze on.

"Dad, what do you think I should do?" I asked him. "You haven't said anything." There was a long pause. Somehow, I managed to stay silent. That was my father. There were usually long silences before he spoke.

"I don't know," he said finally. "But I will support you in whatever you choose to do." I was back to being on my own. It was only after his death that I found out that he felt the same way I did—that America was just too far away.

My mother said I should go and speak to Swamiji, and so I went to my teacher's ashram. I wanted to ask him what he thought I should do. I wanted to get his blessing to leave, but I also wanted him to tell me not to go. The sun was still bright, but there was a chill in the air. Soon, the lights of the *diyas*—little earthen lamps filled with oil and cotton wicks—would twinkle on the river as people came to the bank for evening prayers. I loved watching the evening chants fill the air and the lights swaying over the darkening water. But this time I was not there in peace. I was angry over the circumstances of my life and had come to see my teacher about it. He glanced at me, and sensing my mood, immediately sent me to one of his disciples, showing no interest in hearing what I had to say. As I look back, I can see that this was how I was being taught.

A woman came and led me to a one-room cottage on the grounds of the ashram. The room was bare, with just a bed, a lamp, and a small table. She motioned for me to sit on the floor and left. I sat quietly, cross-legged and uncomfortable. My teacher's disciple was meditating and did not appear to notice my presence. I was angry and resentful. "How is sitting here going to resolve anything?" Yet, I had no choice but to sit.

My attention wandered all over the room, to the picture of my teacher on his disciple's table, to the sandals on the floor. There was nothing there to really occupy me. I don't remember how long I sat there, but I didn't dare disobey my teacher and leave. As I continued to sit, gradually my whole being was filled with peace. Deep and profound peace! And I wasn't even meditating. The peace was palpable and filled the room. When I finally left after touching his disciple's feet, I felt at peace with my life. My teacher's disciple showed me that if I could *shift my vibration*, I could be at peace and bring peace into my world. I had his answer. I had often wondered why Indian teachers sit and meditate instead of actively changing the world around them. I now know that when you are not at peace, the world around you cannot be at peace. Peace begins from within; change begins from within.

The true masters often say, "I have come to give, only to give. But few ask for what I really have come to give." Indian devotees, like devotees all over the world, supplicants at the doors of the divine, have endless wishes to be fulfilled, and they are generally the wrong wishes. Also, there are charlatans, too, that prey on our doubts and insecurities, and we need to weigh these experiences against our own judgment and gut feelings. The amazing part of being around an enlightened teacher who is immersed in the Divine is that they teach without words. They teach in

stories—or even in silences. And when they do speak, sometimes it can be years before we really understand what they truly
want us to learn and understand. Despite being surrounded by
the presence of faith and meeting my teacher, I still had to go on
my own long journey to find out what I was really searching for.

My teacher's silence didn't, however, stop me from hoping the American embassy would turn down my visa. In fact,
I hoped that I would be denied entry into the US each time I
went home to India during the course of my doctoral studies
so that I could just stay home and blame it on someone else.
But that never happened, and I continued to feel suspended over
the Atlantic between India and the United States. When I finally
graduated, my husband insisted we go for the graduation cere-
mony. There were no parents or siblings of the four of us who
were getting our doctorates that day, and so we celebrated our
long-awaited milestones by cheering for each other.

Somewhere, while doing my doctorate, I stopped keeping
in touch with my teacher. I found it hard to trust, to surrender
completely. By the time I thought of my teacher and felt his presence in my life again, he was no longer in his body.

His grace, nevertheless, gave me a glimpse of the invisible
world. Haripriya and my mother too were both teachers, story-
tellers, seers, and makers of miracles. Haripriya fed my appetite
for faith in the invisible as a child through her stories, and now,
as an adult, I narrate these same stories to my own children. I
delight in telling and retelling them; they are vehicles for teaching. And like my mother, I take the fragments and stories of my
life and weave them into a coherent and continuous ribbon of
faith for my children.

In that liminal space—on the threshold of two worlds that
aren't even your own—is a space of low visibility. You have to

make your way forward without knowing where you are going. It is a place of questions without answers. What lies beyond the darkness? What lies beyond the horizon that I cannot see? This is a space of mystery and fear at first, and later, of growth, of faith, and finally of service.

For many years, people would ask me what brought me to America, and I would reply, somewhat humorously, "Providence!" In America, I met my husband, and we got married while we were students. While I never wore the saris or jewelry that my mother had collected for me, I still never imagined that I wouldn't ever really return to the country of my birth. They say you never stand in the same river twice. India changed, my parents grew older, and I changed too.

For a while, life in America looked stable, successful, and comfortable. I graduated and left Rhode Island to spend several years working in international economic policy, focusing on steadily climbing the ladder of achievement. My dream looked like the American Dream. But that too was going to change. My son was born and by the time he was a toddler, I realized that I was struggling to balance work, family, and our dual careers, both with constant travel. I finally surrendered the job I loved to move with my family to Chicago to find that elusive work–life balance. Little did I know that it would take revisiting the traditions of my people to find it.

## — THREE —

# From Fate
# to Destiny

We drove into Chicago in the wee hours of the September morning, our possessions packed tightly into our car. I had arrived in a new city with no work, no friends, and nothing to look forward to. Having left a job I loved to follow my husband's career, I also wanted to focus on a better work–life balance. However, the education and degrees I had accumulated did not prepare me for the disappointment, loneliness, and heartache caused by the downshifting of my career, or the effect it would have on my identity. I was lost. Slowly, I began the journey back to myself—but what was the path forward? Where was I to start? I entered a search for belonging in this new place, exploring my new neighborhood, hoping to meet people and make friends.

On an impulse, I registered for an online homeopathy course, but I found no motivation to even open the study materials. I did sign up for a study group for students in my new city, though, hoping to connect with other people.

It turned out there were only two people in the study group: Colette and me. We didn't live far from each other, so we met for tea because she wanted to discuss some of the remedies and case studies. We discovered that our sons had been born only a few weeks apart. I remember saying, "What a coincidence!"

Colette laughed. "There are no coincidences," she said.

"She's really unusual," I told my husband after that first meeting. "I don't know if this friendship is going to work out."

Yet, I loved Colette. I loved her outlook on life, her sunny disposition, and her laugh. She was interested in astrology, Chinese medicine, and homeopathy. I had never met anyone like her in all the years I had lived in the US—*and* our boys loved playing together.

Two years later, when I was wheeled into the emergency room of the local hospital for heavy uterine bleeding, Colette was by my side. This was my third time in the ER for severe bleeding. I had had a miscarriage that was terminated and then a repeat procedure for the same miscarriage. Now here I was again. My gynecologist had already told me that this had never happened in her twenty-five years of practice, and other gynecologists I had visited gave me no assurances that I would be okay with the limited treatment options they could offer. But I wanted assurances and reassurances.

As I lay there, Colette held my hand. At one point, she asked me, "How many times do you want to go through this before you are willing to try something different?"

I looked up at her. I knew what she was going to say.

"What do you have to lose?" she asked me.

With blood flowing out of me like water, and no hope in sight, I nodded.

A week later, I found Dr. Guo. He practiced Chinese medicine in an office across Chicago. He sat across from me, his face calm, his eyes kind and gentle. He took my pulse.

"Will I be all right?" I asked.

"You will be fine," he said. His voice was soft, but firm; there was no hesitation, just quiet conviction as he looked at me directly. Tears rolled down my cheeks and I heaved a sigh of relief. I knew in that instant that I trusted him. I felt safe and hopeful. I went outside and noticed the lucky bamboo, the Chinese cat beckoning through the window, and the fat smiling Buddha laughing at me. I waited till they assembled my medicines. Within a few weeks, I started to recover. It was so imperceptible that I almost didn't notice how my energy started to come back and my spirits started to lift. Healing makes no sound. It has a silence as it smoothly and gently makes its way through your body, through your bones, through your mind, seeping into your cells. There were no dramatic shifts in tempo with opening bars that proclaimed tomorrow would be different.

## Discovering Flower Essences

The great thing about having young kids is that they are a passport to your neighborhood and community. One day I was in the car with the kids and Ariana, a new mom that I had met, on our way to dinner. We were late for our dinner reservation, and it was clear that we wouldn't get there on time.

"Which way should we go? Should we take the back road?" asked Ariana.

Being unfamiliar with certain parts of Chicago, I had no idea.

"Okay, I'll muscle test and see which way we could go."

I had no idea what Ariana was talking about, but I was completely fascinated. She did something with her hands and chose a way to go. We did reach the restaurant, and there was indeed less traffic the way she chose. At least, that's what it looked like to me. I wanted to know more! Muscle testing looked like the perfect way to make all kinds of decisions. The perfect answer to all my insecurities about choices. Having forayed into Chinese medicine, I was now more open to different healing modalities, so I asked her where I could learn about it. She recommended a holistic health store in Evanston, Illinois.

As it happened, I would drive by this little natural store on Main Street in Evanston on my way to and from work to the daycare and everywhere else. You had to pass Main Street wherever you went: it had the bakery, the toy store, the hardware store, and anything else you might need. She was recommending this same exact place! Now I knew that it was fated that I was going to step into this store and meet its amazing, helpful staff.

"I want to learn about muscle testing," I said to Linda, who worked there. She didn't seem fazed by my question.

Without skipping a beat, she said, "Well, we don't really have a book about muscle testing, but there's a book here that talks about flower essences, and it refers to kinesiology."

I bought the book on the spot. It was hard to read, and I didn't "get" muscle testing. It wasn't easy to learn, but I was intrigued by flower essences. I went back the next day and found Linda again.

"I'd like to find out more about flower essences," I told her.

Linda pointed to some shelves lined with little brown bottles. Their archival, cream-colored labels held intriguing descriptions, such as:

> *Mustard: brings back joy and cheerfulness when gloom descends for no obvious reason*
>
> *Mimulus: brings courage and calm to face things that frighten or worry you, also aids the shy and timid*

Linda explained that these were flower essences, distilled from live flowers. Each essence healed a certain emotional imbalance.

As I touched the bottles, I could feel something resonate within me—just holding them made me calmer. I bought a couple of essences and began learning about this energy medicine for addressing emotional imbalances. Just like with the Chinese medicine I had taken, there were imperceptible shifts in my outlook on life. I began to be more positive and feel less like a victim of circumstance. That was the beginning of my love affair with the essences. Yes, I did learn muscle testing, finally, but not until a decade and a half later . . . and after I had delved deeply into learning about the essences.

I wasn't allowed any shortcuts!

But, into this world of flowers, I was given permission to enter—not as a botanist or an artist, but as a translator between human emotions and nature, learning the language of the essences. Despite my inadequacy for the task ahead of me, the strength of the flowers supported me on every step of my journey.

"You're so interested in the essences, why don't you consider taking this course in California?" asked Linda, since by now I had become a frequent visitor to that section of the store.

I looked at the flier Linda was holding out. I had begun teaching at the university shortly after we moved, and there seemed to be no room for the *heart* within the hallowed halls of academia, so I was already hiding my interest in the essences. However, as soon as I saw the essence course, I knew that I wanted to go, but I didn't know how I would manage it. After dithering till the last few weeks, I finally decided that my whole family would all go to California and make it a vacation. I sent in my application and was accepted.

The day after I was accepted, my friend Jennifer stopped by my home with a load of boxes in her arms.

"These are for you," she said, setting them down on the dining room table. "Flower essences."

There were dozens. They had belonged to a flower essence practitioner who had passed away recently, and her son learned of my interest through Jennifer. I had inherited over a hundred flower essences overnight, for which I was deeply grateful. Although I felt I was about to start my journey, I think many parts of it—even though I didn't realize it at the time—had already been put in place.

"I wouldn't recommend going with your family, though. It's going to be pretty intense," said Jennifer, who had worked with flower essences herself for many years. I couldn't imagine what was going to be so intense that I wouldn't want my family with me. But summer Little League baseball and collusion by the angels found me on my way to Terra Flora, home of the Flower Essence Society, all by myself.

With no background in healing, or anything remotely related to the field, I was pretty certain that I had got into the course because they must have been trying to fill it up. Nevertheless, I took the flight to Sacramento and upon landing, got on the shuttle that took me from the airport to Nevada City, a few miles from Terra Flora. A woman with short, untidy hair came and sat down next to me.

"Do you know how long the shuttle takes to Nevada City?" I asked.

"We should be there in an hour and a half. Are you going to Terra Flora?"

When I nodded, she told me she was wait-listed for the course.

"You're lucky that you got in. I took too long to decide. But I'm on my way to see a friend who's flown in from Japan for the course."

We chatted for a while, and I was humbled to hear that I had made it into the course in the nick of time. I never saw her again, but my life was about to change in ways I could never have imagined.

Terra Flora is a wildlife sanctuary and wildflower preserve in the foothills of the beautiful Sierra Nevada in California. It is also the home and office for Flower Essence Services. Here, Richard Katz and Patricia Kaminski create and research flower essences with their committed staff. Far from pollution, on this wildflower preserve, flowers are grown and made into essences. But Terra Flora is also an enchanted garden. I fell in love with it as soon as I entered. Flowers intertwined with garden angels, a statuary, a sundial, and a bubbling fountain, and open green spaces held welcoming leafy trees. Set amid the rolling hills, their house seemed integrated with the land, open to the sky and light.

Each day, tables were generously laden with lunch for the participants on the wooden deck. You could fill your plate and sit anywhere—under the shady trees, curl up in the library or a corner nook, explore their books, perch on a windowsill, or sit with others at a table. Only their bedroom was off-limits. It amazed me that this was their private home, but we could treat it like our own little refuge.

Although I had always seen my parents keep an open house, Patricia and Richard allowed their house to be overrun by complete strangers. Patricia's warmth was evident, while Richard was a little quieter. Together, their compassion created space for everyone.

Over the week, stories would emerge from the participants: a woman had lost her only daughter in a tragic accident, a young man had been abused as a child, others searched for direction. We each had a story—although I didn't think I had one.

The staff at Terra Flora seemed to love their work. Classes were held in a room that overlooked the gardens, but we also spent a lot of time outside. It was such a sharp contrast to time spent in windowless seminar rooms or university offices and classrooms under artificial light. This was a different kind of work and learning space.

I recognized some of the flowers from my own garden. Up here, though, in the Sierra Nevada, I was introduced to them as if for the very first time. We would walk to the edge of the grounds or hike in the mountains to see them growing. We sat near the plants to see if we could pick up on their subtle qualities, to understand that in a connected Universe, there was communication across species. I sat next to an enormous sunflower. As I tuned into its energy, closing my eyes and breathing evenly, I felt a sense of peace.

Just as we sat near the flowers, closely observing them, their colors, their petals, their leaves, we also learned to be near the essences themselves, to hold them and feel their energetic vibration. Sometimes I do that with my clients too: I ask them to close their eyes and hold the essence near their heart or solar plexus. I might hear the words, "I feel calmer" or "I can feel my heart racing." While their responses may differ, they do feel something. Sometimes flower essence practitioners write that an essence will fall off the table or come to their attention in another way—calling out to be included in a formula. We learn to trust subtle signs.

## The Threshold of Life and Death

At Terra Flora, I experienced the world of flowers, but I also learned something else: I became aware of the importance of life transitions, thresholds from one space to the next.

While I was attending the flower essence course at Terra Flora, my father's health had been deteriorating, and I was deeply concerned. *Will he die? Will I see him again?* When I would speak with my mother on the phone, she worried that he wasn't eating and was getting weaker and that he slept a lot. From what I know now, these are symptoms that the soul is getting ready to depart the body. At that time, I would wake up in the middle of the night, anxious, praying for him to be well. I was filled with fear and sadness; I was not prepared for what happened at Terra Flora.

It was daytime and the sun was streaming through the windows of the warm wood-paneled room that looked out onto the serene gardens. Patricia was speaking about the journey of the soul. I was drifting into a sense of wonder about being there. Suddenly, I felt my father's presence in the room. I felt something was happening—I felt his distress. It made no sense—my father was in India where my parents lived, and it was nighttime there. Anxiety rose up within me. Why was I feeling him here? And why did this sense of his presence make me uncomfortable?

After the workshop session I was attending ended, I called my mother. She told me my father had been hospitalized that day because he had trouble breathing. I felt as if I couldn't breathe myself and went and sat under a tree to compose myself; I wondered how long he had to live.

As I sat there, Marlene, another workshop participant, walked over and asked if she could sit with me. Her calm, kind presence and gentle voice felt like a soft breeze.

I found myself telling her about the call, my voice breaking, trying to hold back the tears.

"Can I share something with you, even though it might sound crazy?" she asked. I nodded, unable to speak. She had already described herself as an energy healer, although I had little idea what that meant. Now she said she felt the presence of a man near her, then saw his fleeting image, describing a tall and thin frame, drawing her shoulders forward to show the way he stood. It was my father.

"He is an old soul," she said, as gently as she could, "and the time has come for him to go."

At that moment, I was only frightened, distraught at the thought of losing my father. Marlene spoke some words of comfort and later that day created a flower essence combination especially for my father. As she handed it to me, she said that Consciousness spoke to her through her faith, guiding her in putting together this "protection" essence that I could use to clear his chakras, or energy centers, on his spine and at the crown. I had heard about chakras but did not know much about them. And I wondered how I would use this essence for my father all the way in India if his time had already come. But maybe it wasn't too late.

Marlene seemed to think so. "Give it to him once a day, for twenty-one days," she said. "You and your mother must take it too!" Three and a half weeks is typically how long a bottle of flower essence lasts. I carefully wrote down her instructions, hoping that this would help him somehow. If I could do something that could change the situation, I was going to do it.

I had already bought my ticket to go to India and planned to fly out a few weeks later. What struck me about her instructions was that I was set to stay there, in India, for exactly twenty-two days. We used the protection essence for twenty-one days, and I left on the twenty-second day.

That trip would be the last time I spent time with my father while he could still speak to me. Although he could hardly even stand or climb the stairs, he wanted to feed my two-year-old daughter. His hand was unsteady as he tried to feed her in her highchair. We celebrated her second birthday in India with him, all of us, for the very last time. The taxi was waiting to take us to the airport. I suddenly remembered that I wanted to take a photograph. That is the last picture I have of him, my mother, and my two children.

## My Lifeline

On the day we arrived back in Chicago from India, the power was out. A massive tornado had swept through the city and its surrounding areas the night before. Broken branches were strewn on the roads, and the power lines in my neighborhood were down. We packed in the available light, and in two days, with heavy hearts, we left Chicago for Boston—our new home. The tornado was a precursor to my own darkness of death, dislocation, and despair.

How did Marlene's essences help my father? A few weeks before he passed away, he made an unexpected trip to his ancestral childhood area several hours away with his nieces and nephews. He insisted on going, even though he was unwell. Perhaps he was connecting back to his roots. It was a place I had never seen, and a place that he too had not returned to since their family lands had been confiscated by a new law and a new government when he was young. That night, tired from the trip, he fell badly but did not break any bones. Perhaps his soul was now prepared to leave his body. A few days later, he was hospitalized.

I returned to India again, six weeks after I had gone back to the US. An oxygen mask covered most of my father's face, and the doctor had told us that he had very little time left. I and other family members gathered around his bedside. He looked frail, but his eyes showed me that he was aware of everything, just as he always had been. He was the one everyone in the extended family turned to for advice and support. With his eyes, he bid each of us farewell. He was ready to go. Life is lived between the first inhalation and the last exhalation. Did the flower essences help prepare him for this transition? I now know that they did.

With his death, the ground below my feet opened up. In the two years that followed my father's death, his entire generation would pass away. There were four deaths in quick succession. Death is a threshold, just as Patricia had said. For me too. I lost not just my father, and beloved members of a generation before me, but with my move to Boston, I also lost my identity again, my network of friends, and in some ways, I lost my mother too as she reeled under the shock of multiple family deaths. With the relocation, my husband was immersed in the requirements of his new position, and my son was adjusting to a new school. I was the emotional caretaker for those I loved, and although I needed support myself, I did not know how to ask for it. If Chicago had been a hard transition, the move to Boston was even more so.

Fortunately, there was a glimmer of hope, although I didn't know it then. I had already signed up to learn about flower essences and had been assigned a mentor. The essences became my lifeline.

With the help of my mentor, instead of running away from my emotions, I began to identify, journal, and learn about them.

I unfailingly took four drops, four times a day from my little dosage bottle; the essences helped me recover more than any visit to a doctor. That inner turmoil that did not show up in any blood tests or symptoms found a space to express itself and received help from the flowers.

I began to be aware that despite my grief over my father's death, there was a sense of completeness in my relationship with him. Though he couldn't speak at the end, there was nothing left unsaid or undone. Nothing needed to be repaired or forgiven. Much as I missed him, I was also at peace.

## Finding My Purpose

Death seems like a separation, and yet those we love, and perhaps even those family members that we don't, continue to live within us. Our task is to honor them and also separate ourselves from them. Often, we seek permission, perhaps even subconsciously, to separate ourselves.

While my father was alive, I could not bring myself to give up my Indian citizenship. Years after he had passed, my mother suggested that I become a US citizen because, as she put it, "America has given you so much." It was in some ways a permission to separate. It was a bittersweet moment when I surrendered my Indian passport.

In India, we have a ritual that gives us permission to separate while honoring our family. Both my grandfathers died before I was born, so we would visit my grandmothers who lived in different cities. Each time, my sister and I had to touch their feet before we left. It was customary in my culture and a gesture of respect for those older than us. When my father's nieces and nephews came to visit my parents, they would always touch their feet too. When the time came to go, they would touch them again. The symbolism of touching an elder's feet softened a departure; it was also a way of receiving their blessing. Looking back on this custom from my very different life now, I can see how it helped me learn to honor the elders in my family, while at the same time separating myself from them. America is an individualistic culture, yet we are not islands. As social creatures, when we experience disconnection, we also experience feelings of anxiety, loneliness, and perhaps even depression. Yet, we are required to individuate in order to honor our soul. Through rituals in this book, you too can learn how to individuate without guilt, or the subconscious desire for permission, while still honoring all that you are part of.

After years of research and teaching economics, I began to feel that the answers didn't lie in that field. There seemed to be a contradiction between the economists' view of a world of scarce resources and an abundant Universe. I found it hard to reconcile the idea of actions governed by self-interest when values of love, compassion, and sacrifice were what I saw my parents live by. What I saw as material poverty was not a poverty of the spirit, and material success could still be accompanied by a poverty consciousness within. In the end, the tension was strong enough to cause me to leave economics altogether. Despite the comforts of a material life, it was not enough to fulfill me. Flower essences, family energy fields—maybe that's what I really came to learn. However, I had to leave home to come back to my ancestors— and to myself.

## — FOUR —

# Discovering Family Energy Fields

As my flower essence practice began to thrive, I realized with client after client that there were patterns that persisted intergenerationally—many were struggling with similar issues their parents had also faced. For instance, the woman who jilted her fiancé had a child who suffered almost the same heartbreak. Another client who didn't speak to her own mother struggled with communication issues with her daughter. Some patterns were obvious, and some were insidious, but all appeared barely perceptible to those affected. Sometimes I saw patterns repeat at similar intervals, such as a move to divorce after the same number of years of marriage, or at the same age that parents had divorced.

All of this showed me how wounds were transmitted through generations. In each instance, there was something in a family that kept getting passed down—something that was calling for resolution and healing.

Around this time, I also started to notice patterns in my own life such as the fact that my mother, sister, and I all lived in cities that we had not grown up in—each of us had married and moved. In these new environments, we faced similar issues of not belonging or not identifying with the dominant culture. And while the circumstance of leaving your childhood village or city in adulthood was not unusual, each of us had moved to a place that was culturally very different from where we had been raised. This was a pattern carried down from generations before me, extending back to my grandmother.

As I became more aware of these patterns, I went to meet Jerry, a friend, holistic practitioner, and philosopher. Jerry was kind, insightful, and wise, much like the Merlin figurine with flowing white hair that shared space with the volumes that lined his bookcases.

"Am I going crazy, Jerry?" I asked. "Am I just imagining something?"

He listened intently and wrote down two names—Emily Blefeld and Dan Booth Cohen.

"I suggest you see them."

They practiced family constellation therapy and lived in Providence—my life had come full circle, back to the place where I had arrived in America many years ago!

At the time, I had no idea what family constellation therapy was. I discovered that it was based on the idea that family was not just a nuclear entity of mother, father, and siblings, but an energy field that goes back many generations—not just grandparents and direct progenitors, but all other sorts of relatives, dead and alive. This field affects us in a myriad of ways. This family energy field has specific principles that govern it, and we pay the price when some member violates them.

Family constellation therapy was pioneered by Bert Hellinger, a German monk and missionary. He was born in Germany in 1925 and worked as a missionary in South Africa, where he lived for sixteen years. It was there that he was exposed to the customs and rituals of the Zulus that influenced his thinking. Finally, after twenty-five years of being a priest, Hellinger left the religious order, returned to Germany, married, and began training as a psychoanalyst.

Although the name of his method sounds like psychotherapy, similar to flower essences, it is really an energy-based approach to healing, one that drew heavily from Hellinger's time in Africa.

As Dan Cohen, Ph.D., author and family constellation facilitator, writes in his book, *I Carry Your Heart in My Heart*, "Family constellation is not a religious ritual or a spiritual practice. It has nothing to do with astrology or stars. It ventures into territory that religion and therapy avoids." By working with this family energy field, Emily and Dan helped their clients find insight, healing, and peace.

## What Is a Family Constellation?

A family constellation is most often carried out in a group setting. Participants or witnesses sit in a circle with an empty space in the center for the constellation process. When I first walked in to see Dan and Emily, there were chairs positioned on the periphery of the carpet. Emily and Dan sat in two of the chairs, and the rest of the participants sat in the others. The carpeted space in the middle was left empty.

The process began with Emily asking the client at the time, a woman I will call Christine, what issue or problem she wanted to address. Christine said her body felt tense and she feared rejection. She felt that she was always ready to erupt any time as if there were a volcano simmering within her.

"Pick someone to represent you and another person to represent the volcano," Emily said to Christine. Just as I had mapped emotions onto flowers in my essence practice, Emily and Dan mapped words onto the constellation process, putting a representative in for the word "volcano"—sometimes transpersonal concepts such as wealth or illness might be added to the constellation. Christine looked around the room and requested two people, one to represent her and another the volcano. Choosing someone to represent her in the circle allowed Christine to be a witness to the situation by observing it with some distance.

In family constellation therapy, since the family itself is viewed as an energy field, the process does not require actual members of the family to be present. Usually, the constellation starts with a few representatives and then more "family members" are added as it proceeds. Individuals step in to represent members of the family, dead or alive. Once inside the circle, emotions, thoughts, and feelings come to the representatives through the family energy field. Just as I had felt the energy of the plant simply by sitting next to it in Terra Flora, I noticed that participants picked up on the energy of the family members once they stepped into the circle. They could feel what the individual family members feel. As the representatives move, it seems as if the energy of the family field starts to guide their direction.

We all watched to see how the "volcano" and "Christine" representatives interacted with each other. The volcano was actually joyous and danced within the circle and around "Christine."

"Let's put someone in for your mother and father," said Dan.

As we put in more participants, family dynamics began to come to light. Christine's "mother" was not demonstrably affectionate and kept a tight leash on her daughter's behavior. This was evident from the way she stood and her body language.

What became starkly clear was that when Christine's "mother" entered the circle, the "volcano" immediately started to whimper and retreat. Christine's "father" seemed to be somewhat protective of "Christine," and she seemed to hide behind him. The "volcano" stayed in the corner. It became clear that this was Christine's inner reaction to her mother.

Emily showed Christine that she was cowering before her mother and afraid to express herself. Christine also acknowledged that the representations corresponded to the dynamics of interaction in her family. Dan then introduced Christine's grandmother into the constellation. We noticed the same pattern of aloofness and control between the "grandmother" and Christine's "mother." Even though Christine's grandmother was not alive, it was possible to see her emotional imprint in the body language of the representative.

We learned that Christine's grandmother had experienced the horror of war and through the constellation, we could see how this affected the nature of parenting available to Christine's mother as well as Christine. It's almost as if through the constellation, Christine could see the backstory that had created her mother into the person she was. She saw her grandmother's behavior as the result of the trauma she had lived through. She saw her mother's behavior as the result of the parenting she had received. If the constellation had gone further back into the lineage, we might have had insight into the incidents that shaped Christine's progenitors even further back than her grandmother. However, for now, the constellation did create this moment when Christine could look at the family situation that unfolded before her eyes so she could see her family story in a new way. As Christine saw the patterns of behavior, this awareness elicited compassion for her parents and her grandmother.

Emily and Dan focus on what is happening in the circle in order to address the issue the client has come to deal with. Dan, in his book, *I Carry Your Heart in My Heart*, explains that when we find ourselves struggling with a problem that seems to have no solution, the lens through which we are viewing the problem may be too narrow. Christine could now understand the feelings of rejection and anxiety she was carrying in the context of her family history—the result of the trauma of war and the control her mother exercised on her behavior. Dan often said, when we ask the question, "Whose problem was it before it was ours?" we open ourselves to the field of our ancestors and to grace and healing.

The family energy field has already come together to heal the family situation that has presented itself. It needs the skill of the facilitator to make space for the insight that wants to reveal itself, and this is the insight that will make healing for the client possible. With the aid of the representatives, Dan and Emily provide that insight. As skilled facilitators, they track the room, each nuance of the representatives, their body language, and words. Along with years of experience, both Emily and Dan have flashes of intuition that also guide this process.

A key aspect of this process is that the client is able to see the situation from the perspective of other family members as well as their own. As Christine discovered, a family constellation also allows clients to discover the impact of the trauma their family might have experienced and how this might have led her to feel the way she did.

I was fascinated because while I knew which essences could help Christine, I also now saw the origin of the feelings Christine experienced. I became aware of the repetition of patterns of behavior, such as control, and emotions such as feelings of rejection and anxiety in her lineage and what might have caused them.

Emily invited me to join a year-long training in family constellations with them. I didn't really understand how healing happened in a constellation, but I wanted to learn. I wanted to ascertain what lay behind the repetition of patterns and the emotions we experience. We are all on a journey inward to heal ourselves and the subconscious patterning we carry, and I felt that this training would help me and my flower essence clients. Watching and participating in different constellations, I began to see the similarities between issues that different people faced, and I also discovered that there were principles that governed the family energy field.

Every other month, I would drive to Rhode Island on Thursday evening for a long weekend. Emily and Dan rented two adjacent houses on the waterfront. Workshops were held in one, and meals were served in the other. Participants came from all over the world—New Zealand, Canada, Europe, and as far off as Hawaii and Washington State. Sometimes, the constellations went on for hours. We might have been tired or hungry, but what was going on before our eyes held us riveted. I ended up training with them for two years. In the process, pieces of myself were being put back together—like a puzzle. I was finally seeing a connection between flower essences and family constellations and being led back to my own roots.

## Whose Emotions Are We Carrying?

Family constellations are based on the concept that some of the emotions we experience may not have originated with us personally. Emotions are not just messengers of our pain—they are messengers from the family energy field. For instance, trauma can shift the parenting response. The constellation showed that both the grandmother and mother were very controlling, and Christine's feelings of anxiety and rejection were a response to that trauma passed down through the generations. It's possible that Christine's mother and grandmother may have used control over their children to hide their own feelings of anxiety and rejection. The healing Christine experienced in the constellation reflected the desire of the family energy field to support her.

There is scientific evidence that emotions are transmitted across generations. In 1966, the late Dr. Vivian Rakoff, a professor of psychiatry at the University of Toronto, was the first to observe that many of the children of Holocaust survivors had emotional responses similar to their parents. In April 2015, in an article in the *Globe and Mail* written by Ian Brown, "The Holocaust's Long Reach: Trauma Is Passed On to Survivors' Children," Dr. Rakoff is quoted as saying, "It would almost be easier to believe that they, rather than their parents, had suffered." Some children of Vietnam War veterans were also observed to have heightened levels of stress similar to their parents', even though they themselves had not gone to war. This same article went on to discuss that there is now growing evidence that children are affected by the trauma their parents were exposed to before their birth and even possibly before they were conceived.

I'm often struck by the power of strong, cruel, vengeful words to reverberate through time, which are almost like curses spoken out loud. In family constellations, we can watch the stories of our lives as if we are watching a play. Just as in constellations, in sessions with clients, I hear the words they have been told—carried now in their hearts for a long time. These words stand out as if hanging in the air, waiting to be plucked.

"I never loved you!"

"I wish you were never born!"

"I never wanted you!"

Like a knife plunged deep into our hearts, they leave their mark for all time. Through family constellations, I discovered words and phrases like these reflected the unconscious past that reached out into the present. For example, the unwanted pregnancy a generation before appears connected to the unwanted child in the present one, or disappointing relationships in one generation manifest as unrequited and unexpressed love in the next. These words point to the unresolved trauma or wound that exists in the family system, expressing itself in the words the client hears. After I started observing family dynamics in family constellations, it seemed that reality was more dramatic than fiction, paling in comparison against a vast family saga. Past and present mingled—those who were alive were trapped in the drama of those long gone.

I was drawn to family constellation therapy like a moth to a flame. The constellation, as each group process is called, fascinated me. I would return again and again, even traveling to watch other facilitators in family constellation work. What struck me most about family constellation work was its focus on healing the family relationships that may have led to emotional patterns of rejection, anxiety, and grief, oftentimes leaving the client with a sense of abandonment.

Family constellation therapy shone a light on family drama—one of understanding, compassion, and forgiveness—a higher-order healing energy. Light and dark were two sides of the same coin. Similar to flower essences, family constellations also attempted to expand our emotional range by shifting negative emotions.

Emily and Dan would say there are no accidents: those who were chosen to represent family members often found that the client's story might resonate in their own families. Representing in a constellation is considered an act of service to the family energy field—not just the client's but your own—because as you shift, you shift your ancestral energy field. For those of us who were watching a constellation, it was as if we were being taught lessons about life by the ancestors in each lineage. Each time I came home from a constellation weekend, I came back a little brighter, wiser, kinder, and more humble.

As I tried to make sense of what I was seeing and experiencing, there was an integration happening in my heart. My mother's family lived in Assam, the eastern part of India, and owned tea plantations. There were many British plantations as well, and the lifestyle of the British was evident to the local people. Into this environment, my mother was born. Although my grandfather held out against the British lifestyle, his eldest daughter left her father's home to study in Calcutta. This was an enormous departure for a man who had never left Assam. One by one, the remaining children followed suit. When my grandfather died, my uncle was forced to take over the running of the tea plantation. However, while he tried to emulate the British plantations, the tea plantation suffered financially, and the story had a tragic ending.

My father, on the other hand, grew up in a town that had the largest British cantonment in India. It was here the unsuccessful mutiny by Indian soldiers against the British began in 1857. The mutiny was bitterly squashed, and greater separation grew between the two lifestyles. Despite glimpses of the British lifestyle, his family had strong Indian roots.

North India, where I was raised, has been exposed to hordes of marauding armies over centuries, so the women are traditionally protected and secluded. This entangled polarity represented by my parents' vastly different heritages was the climate of my childhood—westernization and tradition—and their shadows. I started to become aware of how my own deep-seated beliefs were shaped by multiple forces way before my time—that reached back into India's colonial past.

This history was within me, and I would have to make my way forward in the crossfire of its conflict, unaware of how I was always navigating these waters. For instance, in pursuing my version of success, the westernized part of myself lost sight of what truly nourished me—the roots and philosophy of my traditions. Part of this loss came from the way I believed things "should" be, or what I thought I needed to do in order to be successful. And yet, the traditional roles of wife, mother, daughter, and volunteer, in which I had circumscribed myself, were not enough to sustain me.

I was constantly trying to find that elusive balance that would fulfill me. I started to understand my own family history and the forces that had shaped me. Family constellations made me aware of the principles that my parents lived by and what I had grown up with. I started to understand the wisdom of my own traditions that allowed us to honor the departed as well as the veil that lay between us and those who had left. And how this was integral to our peace and well-being.

Yet, although I trained in family constellations, I could not ultimately embrace them—I wanted more energetic distance from other people's ancestral energy fields. How did the world of those departed reach out and affect the living? What was the nature of the pain that had so much power to affect a family?

I learned that the veil between worlds was very, very thin and affected us constantly. I realized that the dead wanted to reach out to the living to make amends, and the living too were reaching out subconsciously to those who had gone, searching for the love that was lost or perhaps never experienced.

Just as flower essences peel away emotions to reveal layers of other emotions underneath, family constellations peel away layers of family history to provide insight into pain. Depending on how far you want to journey on this path, one flower essence or one family constellation may not be enough to heal deep-seated issues. Some people may integrate these insights into their lives easily. For others, more support may be needed. It took me a long time to learn the principles that governed the family energy field and how they operated. I discovered that these cannot be taught in a single constellation. These are often part of a longer training, but these principles provide a road map for the client.

I also realized that the family energy field decides how much will be revealed or healed. In addition, these revelations and how far back the family energy field goes depend on the capacity of the client, the time available for each constellation, and the skill of the facilitator. Facilitators generally don't reveal insights beyond what the client can handle. That usually marks the end of the constellation. It requires a skilled facilitator and grounding, as well as cleansing, techniques to keep our individual energy fields intact so that we do not absorb unwanted energies. While more facilitators are available today in the US than they were a few years ago, they can still be hard to find.

## Karma: The Law of Cause and Effect

As I searched for ways to help my clients, I discovered there were echoes between family constellation work and my own Indian traditions.

From an early age, growing up in an Indian family, I had been taught that all of us are subject to karma, which literally means *action*—physical or mental. In the physical world, Isaac Newton postulated that every action has an equal and opposite reaction. There is a counterpart in the energetic world: an equal and opposite energetic reaction. Indian traditions believe that karmic experiences—things that happen to you in your life—may be the result not only of your own actions but someone else's as well, perhaps going back generations within a family. We have individual karma and also family karma. It might not be evident to us how those actions play out. Yet according to the law of karma, a great-grandmother you never met could have been responsible for the experience you or someone else in the lineage is having today.

When an individual is suffering in some way, it's natural for people raised in my spiritual tradition to assume that events in the past led to the experiences of today. I've heard it said many a time, "As you sow, so shall you reap." What I was seeing in family constellations was the law of karma at play: consequences of actions that affected subsequent generations. However, I didn't understand what these laws or principles were and how they worked. That's what I was learning through constellations. Daniel Foor, Ph.D., a Western-educated psychotherapist, also helps his clients understand that the living and dead strongly affect one another. In his book, *Ancestral Medicine: Rituals for Personal and Family Healing*, he points out that destructive actions by recent ancestors can reverberate through the living family for generations, functioning as a kind of ancestral curse, oppressive transgenerational karma, or pervasive bad luck.

Many people see karma as a fate that they are powerless over. This leads to a feeling of victimhood and an abdication of personal power and responsibility. To me, that's a very disempowering way to look at karma. I have met people who were certain that those who spent their days on the streets of Delhi begging for food and money had inherited their fate. Perhaps many in India don't rebel against their lot in life. But through flower essences and family constellations, I started to think about karma differently. I have come to believe that karma isn't about paying the price for your own or someone else's behavior, and it doesn't have to lead to hopelessness. Karma isn't the punishing force that people believe it to be. You aren't to blame for that ancestor who jilted a suitor, or for the one who couldn't bond appropriately with her children. Karma doesn't get passed down because we deserve to suffer for our own or someone else's actions. While it can be thought of as a principle that rights wrongs by balancing scales energetically, karma also gives us the chance to change old patterns. Through this human form, karma offers us the option to consciously choose what will help us heal, grow, and learn spiritual lessons about life. It does this by presenting us with life events, relationships, and situations that echo the past in some way, whether it's our past or our family's past. If we, as a human race, were no longer present on earth, it would continue to exist without us. We are the ones who need to be present for the evolution of our souls to experience that movement toward connection, harmony, and love—a journey that starts with our family energy field but begs us to extend these feelings to those living today. A challenging adventure!

Through family constellation therapy, I learned so much about transgenerational wounds and how they affect us, and how deeply everything is connected—the land we live on and its history, the cultural forces that impact families, and the struggle through the generations to express love. How easy it was to lose that expression of love. I began to see how family constellation therapy was linked to the Indian concept of karma, and that there were ways to heal karma that existed not just in my tradition, but in other traditions.

This book is intended to help you heal transgenerational trauma and shift patterns through more accessible therapies, which are discussed in Part II. There, I will discuss the role of flower essences, altars, and prayers. These are tools anyone can use to help release the patterns that you have inherited so you can release the past to create the life you want.

## Journal Exercises

1.  Are there patterns of emotions—positive or negative—that run in your family? Are your family members gregarious and outgoing, or reserved with defined boundaries? Are there patterns of depression, anxiety, or aggression that run in your family? Are there traumatic events that your parents might have experienced? If you go back further, do you know something of what your grandparents or great-grandparents might have experienced? If you don't know these stories, don't worry. There's a lot that you can still do, as you will discover in the next few chapters.

2.  Polarity—the presence of opposites—is one way that the Universe draws our attention to what *we need to see*. You might see these polarities, or sharp contrasts, in your life too.

Some instances are perhaps a mother who holds down the steady job, while the father is always pursuing new opportunities that may not always pan out. Or you come from a family that struggled financially and marry into a family of wealth and privilege. When challenges exist, the presence of polarities point to the emotional contradictions you might be struggling with internally. For instance, a part of me was drawn to what was westernized, and a part remained deeply traditional. What polarities do you see in your life or lineage?

# PART II

# Healing Tools

# FIVE

# Healing with Flower Essences

An essence is capturing the most ephemeral, ethereal quality of a flower—the energy of its morning dew—created between the coolness of the night and the warmth of the dawning sun. Dew, since time immemorial, was believed to have magical restorative properties in different cultures all over the world. But clearly, it is challenging to collect enough! Flower essences get as close to that as possible. Flowers are picked just before they are at their peak and floated in a glass bowl that is placed on the earth, or rocks, under a cloudless sky. The flowers cover the surface of the bowl. The alchemy of earth, water, sunlight, and air create a flower essence, energetically imprinting the water with the emotional healing property of the flower. At Terra Flora, where I first experienced the making of flower essences, I saw the water change after a few hours in the sunshine. The quality of the water had shifted, almost as if it had a sparkle; the flowers had released their energy. The flowers themselves are then removed with pincers so that human hands do not touch them, and the water is strained and preserved with brandy. Sometimes, essences are also preserved with non-alcoholic glycerin for those who can't tolerate or want to avoid the use of alcohol. That is how you get a flower essence.

For all their color and beautiful fragrance, flowers do not impart these qualities to their essences. When I say, "I'm a flower essence practitioner," people often respond, "Oh, an aromatherapist." It's easy to assume that flower essences are the same as essential oils, which, like most flowers, have a distinct smell. But essences don't. They are the "energetic" healing essence of the flower and not part of its physical structure. Unlike an essential oil, it is the *energy* of the flower and so to make it, you just use enough flowers to cover the surface of the water. You don't need fields of flowers to create a flower essence like you do with an essential oil. In fact, just a few flowers are enough to create a mother lode of the essence.

The magic of the flowers and the sense of compassion, meaning, and fulfillment that I saw at Terra Flora made me want to be part of this world. Yet, I was also overwhelmed by how many essences there were. How would I know which one to use? Where was I to start? Would I have to test them energetically for myself or others, as I had read in the book that had originally introduced me to flower essences? My rational academic mind needed a framework. I decided to start at the beginning, where it all began—with the Bach flower essences, created by Dr. Edward Bach.

The unique energetic vibrations of different flowers were identified in the 1930s by an English surgeon, Edward Bach, who left his lucrative medical practice and is credited with developing a system of flower essence remedies. Just as certain flowers have been used to heal the physical body, they have also been used to correct emotional imbalances for thousands of years. Papyrus scripts dating back to ancient Egypt point to their use in emotional healing. In the twelfth century, the German mystic Hildegard von Bingen placed muslin sheets over flowers at night. She would wring them out the next day, wet with the morning dew, and then use the water to tend to the emotional needs of the people who came to see her. Lost through time, the energetic healing properties of flowers were again discovered by Dr. Bach almost a hundred years ago. He brought his medical training, as well as subsequent years of research and study in the laboratory, to document and classify the flower essences he created. He also developed a simple method of capturing and stabilizing the healing energy of the flower so that anyone could use them. Since then, multiple case studies have supported Dr. Bach's observations on their emotional healing properties. I began a three-year intensive program to learn about the thirty-eight essences he discovered and their healing properties and became a certified flower essence practitioner. Today, there are several different creators of essences and many more essences in addition to the original ones identified by Dr. Bach. I am most familiar with the Bach essences and those created by the Flower Essence Services in California. However, you are welcome to experiment with others that appeal to you.

The Bach approach was different from Terra Flora. Instead of learning about the journey of the soul and the way the flowers grew and tuning in to their energy as I did at Terra Flora, I learned how to recognize and map emotions onto the flowers using the words my clients spoke.

"My life will never be the same again." Gorse. It restores hope.

"I find it hard to say no to anyone!" Centaury. It helps you set boundaries.

"He makes me so mad! I feel I could explode in an instant." Cherry Plum. It helps you when you fear loss of control.

Flower essences took me into this world of emotions—their nuances, their various names. I learned to look for emotions' telltale clues in the stories and sentences I heard from my clients, which I then connected to particular flower essences. Some flowers are mapped on to feelings of jealousy, despair, anxiety, and fear. They then transform them into love, hope, courage, and faith.

While essential oils are applied topically and can be toxic if taken internally, flower essences are taken orally. Typically, several essences are combined to create a customized bottle since you often have multiple emotions that you are dealing with. You then take four drops, four times a day from the dosage bottle. Once on waking, twice during the day, and again just before going to bed. The drops can be put in your tea, coffee, soup, or just directly in your mouth with the little dropper that comes with the bottle. As I mentioned in Chapter 1, according to neuroscientist Candace Pert, emotions have an energetic frequency almost like radio waves. Each essence works with the energy of the emotion, creating a vibrational resonance that shifts the frequency of the thoughts and emotions you experience.

Despite my intensive study of the essences, the flowers themselves seemed far away, so I decided to visit the Bach Centre in England. I took the train from London to Brightwell-cum-Sotwell in Oxfordshire. Stefan Ball, the author of several books and a Bach educator, greeted me at Dr. Bach's home. It's called Mount Vernon, and this is where Dr. Edward Bach lived and worked in the last years of his life. Stefan showed me around the garden and the rooms of the house, including Dr. Bach's little office. Like Terra Flora, work and life co-mingled with passion, harmony, and devotion. I saw the garden pathways, the flowers themselves, the old bottles, beakers, and labels, and the furniture that Dr. Bach made—even the way his chair was positioned: angled so that the client who came to see him was heard but not overwhelmed. I *felt* the kindness of the keepers of this place, of the garden: those who saw the need for refuge in the world and had enough heart to create it. Even though Dr. Bach died in 1936, these custodians came forward to keep his work alive—each of whom promised to honor the simplicity of his system. Today, the focus of the Centre is education, and they do not make the remedies commercially anymore.

As I stood there marveling at the flowers from the seeds, some of which Dr. Bach himself had planted many decades earlier, I felt humbled and grateful for all that I had received. The seeds he scattered have blown far and wide—there are practitioners all over the world! In addition to the Bach teachers and mentors, I traveled to many places and learned of other essence practitioners. I met a practitioner on a trip to Iceland who showed me the local flowers in her garden. She made her own version of the Bach essences because when she started her practice, she was not allowed to import them. While we walked along the pathways around her house and out into the scrub, she pointed out some of the flowers that she used. It was there, in her serene garden, that I learned about different energy centers in the body—called *chakras* in India—and the way flower essences shift these energies, and that it was possible to "read" trauma that was encoded and stored in the body. However, in the US, we generally only use flower essences to shift emotions, not to treat physical symptoms. On another learning trip, I talked to a midwife in Alaska who had become a flower essence practitioner and she introduced me to Alaskan flower essences, created by Steve Johnson, a former firefighter. Her practice involved flying all over Alaska in seaplanes to provide relief. I discovered

Lila Devi, who created the Spirit-In-Nature flower essences in California. Each of these practitioners inspired me by their lives, their connection with Mother Nature, their authentic calming presence, their unconventional life journeys, and by the work they did helping others.

I became aware of how much nature is there to support and heal us. To this day, I am amazed at how targeted flower essences can be. I still remember holding Pomegranate flower essence at Terra Flora—it was the essence that had called to me then because it was for balancing work and family while honoring your creativity. In fact, the premise of all flower essences is restoring emotional balance. While outer circumstances may not change, with the flower essences, your reaction to them does. It's about coming home to yourself with help from Mother Nature.

Not all essences are from flowers. Rock Water, the only remedy Dr. Bach created that was not from a flower, was from an underground spring. It contained the essence of water—*flow*. Rock Water has the ability to release energetic blocks in the body and the mind. Julian Barnard, author of *Bach Flower Remedies: Form and Function*, says that the remedy can be made from any water untouched by man, suggesting that water has a healing power intrinsic to it. In holy sites like Lourdes, where water flows from a grotto, devotees believe that it has a healing quality. Among the last essences that Dr. Bach discovered was the energetic imprint of flowering trees such as Cherry Plum, Elm, Pine, Beech, Willow, and a few others. He boiled flowering sprays in spring water for thirty minutes in an enamel pan in order to mirror the intensity of the emotional states they treated.

## How Essences Work

Working with the remedies for well over a decade, I am deeply aware of how the remedies shift thoughts, almost effortlessly, to a positive state. While your thoughts may appear to be neutral—they may not in themselves elicit an emotional reaction—your judgments, beliefs, opinions, memories, or past experiences about a situation, person, or event trigger them. Very often, you get stuck and your thoughts keep circling like well-worn grooves in an oft-trodden path. You keep experiencing those old emotions as long as you keep yourself tethered to the same judgments, beliefs, memories, or other subconscious patterns that are running your life—whether it's "She hurt me," or "He should have known his behavior would upset me," or something else. Since it is your thoughts that trigger emotions, the essences essentially shift these negative thoughts—including the ones that are harsh self-judgments.

Since the essences work so gently—and when first taken, there appears to be nothing happening—cynics would have no hesitation in writing them off as placebos. However, with patience, you will find that they are very effective. Here are two simple instances of clients who discovered that the benefits of flower essences can be hard to discern initially. A friend, whose husband worked late into the evening, hated being by herself when her husband was gone and watched television endlessly until he came home. She had no interest in anything and was unable to pull herself away from the television. I gave her Wild Rose for her apathy and lack of interest in doing anything else, and when I saw her next, I asked her how she felt. She said she didn't know and couldn't tell if anything was different. I asked her if she was still watching television every night. She looked a little surprised and admitted that she hadn't watched television for the last couple of weeks. She didn't know why; she simply didn't feel like watching it.

Similarly, a client had a son who was afraid of bees and other insects, which made it difficult for him to tolerate being outdoors. I gave him Mimulus for his fear of insects because he was going on a field trip with his class. When I met his mother a few weeks later, I asked her how his field trip went. She said he seemed a little calmer before and after. Then she told me that a bee had been buzzing around him while he lay on the grass, but he didn't seem to be bothered by it. Although he was too little to notice a difference after taking the essences, his mother did. In these instances, it seems like the essences are doing "nothing," yet, it is in their very gentleness that their strength and effectiveness lie.

If you are mindful, you will notice that your reactions to the events around you change when you take the essences. Working with the remedies has often been likened to "peeling an onion." The outermost layers of emotion are treated first, and once you "peel" these layers, then you move deeper and deeper to work on the more fundamental issues that might be affecting you. According to researchers at the Institute of Neuroscience and Psychology at the University of Glasgow in a study conducted there in 2014, there are four basic emotions: fear, anger, sadness, and joy. These primary emotions are connected in some way to our past: they are how the past surfaces into the present. They are also connected to the way in which you see the future.

Flower essences identify the nuanced nature of the primary negative emotions in order to shift them. They meet you where you are now emotionally, and once those emotions start to shift, others begin to be revealed. The little tag lines on the bottles are only a teaser of what the essences can really do. The more

I worked with them, the more I discovered how powerful they really were.

### Example: What Flower Essences Would Christine Need?

Let's look at a family constellation client, Christine, whose story I discussed in more detail in Chapter 4, to see what flower essences she might need if she was seeking flower essence therapy.

"If I let it all out, I think I'll explode," said Christine. She felt that she was always ready to erupt any time, as if there were a volcano simmering within her. When you ignore or suppress your feelings, they don't go away; they are like a volcano brewing within you. Trying to stop the volcano from erupting takes a lot of your energy, which can make you feel tired and drained. Moreover, pushing down your feelings can cause them to resurface non-verbally through your body language or behavior. There was so much controlling behavior in Christine's family that her analogy was significant—both from the point of view of family constellations as well as from that of flower essences.

Without knowing more than this about her, Cherry Plum, the essence for when you fear losing control, would be indicated since it would help release the tension she was holding.

Christine also said her body felt tense and she feared rejection at the start of the constellation. Reading between the lines, she was searching for greater acceptance or visibility in her relationships. The flower essence for this emotion would be Chicory, to release the need *to be seen*, and its attendant emotions of being acknowledged and appreciated.

I would add Holly for the feelings of anger Christine holds toward her family.

To help her accept herself, I would have investigated her feelings of rejection further. What do they feel like? Several essences present themselves for exploration to be included in her healing formula. Crab Apple—to see how she feels about her physical appearance and its relation to her feelings of rejection. Buttercup—to build her self-worth—or Sunflower—to help her have confidence in being seen. Larch—to give her confidence to take risks and release the feelings of self-doubt and self-censure. All of these essences work slightly differently, but each one can help to bring you to a place of accepting yourself.

The constellation itself pointed to several essences, but the "volcano" whimpering in the constellation strongly pointed to Mimulus—for fear of speaking up. In this way, you can see how flower essences can help you heal the emotions that are transmitted through the generations. As you work through your feelings and the essences in this book, perhaps you can see what essences call to you too. Slowly, you will build the confidence to create your own formula. Since you often have more than one emotion at a time, you can combine several essences to create a unique blend. Dr. Bach suggested combining no more than seven at a time in order to experience their subtle benefits.

Flower essences work not just in dealing with fear, apathy, or regret; they can also help you when you are dealing with transitions and setbacks, as my own experience taught me.

## Essences of Transformation

It was two years since we had left Chicago. Two brokers later, our house still stood forlornly for sale, empty and shuttered. The brokerage For Sale sign hung askew, dangling on its side from one hook as we debated what we should do. "It's the worst recession we've ever seen. Nothing is selling," the brokers told us.

Peter, the new broker I interviewed over the phone, was brash and self-assured. I could almost see the swagger in his gait, the generously sized suits, and the carefully combed-back hair. The price drop he suggested was staggering, but he was confident that his aggressive marketing plan would sell our house in a month.

I could feel the anger welling up in me. Our sweat equity in the house evaporated before my eyes. The long-awaited kitchen and bath renovation had been months of exacting and time-consuming planning and execution. Finally, the soft white cabinets, the green granite and coordinating tile work were ready, but then it had been time to move. Yet, no one else seemed to want the advertised "dream kitchen" and "spa-like" master bath. Tears of frustration and sadness mingled with my anger, sweeping me away in the flood of emotion. The dam had burst. "Let go," I heard a voice inside me say. "Just let go." I hadn't realized before that I was upset about more than just the financial loss. Days later, I picked myself up. I knew I needed the flower essences.

Willow and Honeysuckle gently brought me back to life. Honeysuckle, the striking red trumpet-shaped flower, a clarion call to the present, allowed me to draw my energies back from the past. Willow, flexible to the wind, made me let go of the regret for the life I had not lived, of the garden I had laboriously planted, and the kitchen I barely enjoyed. In my hands, I held the only remembrance of the house that I had saved and carried with me. It was an irregularly shaped piece of green granite—the color of the kitchen countertops. It was bigger than my hand, and little specks of blue danced in it like it does when sunlight hits the ocean. *That's why I had chosen it.* I held it tight and remembered how I had been given a chance to grow through my years in the house, step beyond my comfort zone, and learn to believe the impossible. Then, I remembered bringing each of my children home: my son on a snowy winter night and my daughter on a warm summer afternoon. I thought of all our friends from Chicago that had visited us in our little rental here in Boston, telling me how much they had missed us after we had moved. The Midwest had been kind to us. I made my peace.

I hired Peter and I did the unthinkable. Wild Oat and Scleranthus flower essences guided me to drop the price to the lower of his two proposed numbers. The house sold within a month at a price higher than Peter had believed would be possible, and the new owners fell in love with the kitchen the moment they walked into the house. Their daughter was the same age as mine. I knew the house loved them too; I was able to let go.

## How Long Should You Take Flower Essences For?

You might be wondering how long you should take flower essences. The answer to this question depends on what you are taking them for. Are you going to an important meeting? An audition? A theme park and are afraid of roller coasters? Do you hate flying? Are you struggling to decide between two options? For these immediate situations, you can always take a flower essence, or some targeted combination, that will assist you right away. Are there situations that make you anxious? You could take Rescue Remedy, the popular combination of five flower essences even used by several movie stars. Rescue Remedy provides relief in acute or stressful situations: it supports you, but it does not address long-standing issues to provide deep healing.

If you were to use or create a custom blend for yourself, you would notice a difference in a few weeks, and each customized bottle of flower essences lasts about three and half weeks. However, long-standing issues require essences for a longer period—perhaps a few months or more. For instance, if a long-term relationship has ended and you are deeply upset about it, the essences need to be taken for several months, since there are layers of emotions to be dealt with. Some you may not feel comfortable addressing right away. The essences, in this case, will work layer by layer, providing strength, insight, and learning. Each customized bottle of essences lasts about a month and as emotions shift, you might use different formulations depending on the changes. For instance, when I'm working with a client, I reconsider the formulation each month based on which emotions have shifted, which new underlying ones may have emerged, and which may be the same.

Through my training in flower essences, I learned about the chakras—or energy centers in the body—that create a road map of the journey of the soul. This is not a book about the chakras, so I am only discussing it very briefly here, but there are plenty of ancient Indian and modern books on the chakras, what happens when they are imbalanced, and what balance in each chakra looks like. To give you a very general idea of how they are related to our topic in this book, I can tell you that each chakra governs certain emotions and their physical organs. Family issues are connected to the root chakra, situated energetically at the base of the spine. Unresolved issues here manifest in your relationships with others as well as with yourself. Relationships with others are governed by the second chakra, known as the sacral or sex chakra; your relationship with yourself and your sense of self-worth is governed by the solar plexus chakra. As you heal your family relationships, you heal your relationship with yourself and with others, and you journey up through the chakras with the help of the flower essences. Should you choose to go deeper on this journey and choose this path, the essences provide long-term support as you navigate the twists and turns that lie ahead.

Flower essences can help you if you reach a turning point in your life where you really want to make choices about how you want to live. This is the journey of the soul. When you heal your emotions, you shift your family energy field and heal your roots as well.

## Identify Your Emotions Exercise

Dr. Bach envisaged that every household would have a set of flower essences to turn to, just as you might turn to your medicine cabinets for Band-Aids or Tylenol. If you create a little starter kit for yourself, you can turn to it whenever you need some support.

One of the hardest things to do is to identify how you are feeling. You might be irritable or anxious but not be fully aware of what has triggered your emotions. You might create a connection with others by mirroring them—returning their warmth with a smile or a hug, or being empathetic when needed—but how often do you *connect with your feelings*? Most often, you disconnect from your feelings by ignoring or suppressing them. However, it actually takes a lot of work to keep your feelings at bay.

If you can shift your perception and recognize that these emotions are important messengers about how you have disconnected from yourself or your family energy field, you can learn to honor them. You can start to name the emotions that come up, and slowly, you will begin to understand what triggers the way you feel.

Sit or stand with your feet firmly on the ground. Breathe in and out a few times. Ask yourself, "How do I feel now?" See if you can name the emotion. If you can do this several times a week, notice which emotions come up for you frequently and write these down in your journal to keep a record of them for yourself.

As you work through this book, you will start to identify the emotions and corresponding essences. At the end of the book is a Glossary of essences as well as a short list of essences that you might want to use as a starter kit. I will also list combinations of essences that can be helpful in dealing with issues I discuss.

# — SIX —

# How to Honor
# Your Ancestors

How can you release the unseen patterns that limit your life? Growing up in India in a large family, I saw my relatives often. My father was the youngest of seven siblings, so my many cousins and I spent days flying kites, playing hide-and-seek in the nooks and crannies of my grandmother's home, and eating food from street vendors. My father and uncles helped to take care of my widowed paternal grandmother and conferred together on important family decisions.

One such decision that weighed on the family was the marriage of my oldest cousin. She was to have an arranged marriage and since my aunt was widowed, the responsibility for finding an appropriate match fell on the family as a whole. But nobody could find her an appropriate suitor.

Finally, the family priest or pundit was called in. The problem, he said, was *pitr dosh*, loosely translated as "fault or mistake of the ancestors" that prevented the first marriage in the family from taking place. At some point in the past, in my father's family, ancestral rites had not been performed to fully release the dead. Because of this lapse, the priest said, the family lineage could not continue. Ancestors that are not honored can cause a disturbance in the energy field shared by the entire family, including those living today. It fell to my eldest uncle to perform an ancestral offering to heal this disturbance, even though this was not his daughter. My cousin did get married soon after, and it turned out to be a happy marriage! Now you might dismiss this story as superstition or a coincidence, and when I considered myself a rational economist, I did too. However, today, as I witness changes in my own life and that of my clients, I have come to believe that there is something deeper than what you can see before you affecting your life in very real ways.

Nearly every culture on earth has some ritual for honoring ancestors. Celtic and Norse peoples had well-established traditions to revere their ancestors. In Ireland, the festival of Samhain invited those who had died to feasts at which the souls of the dead had a place set at the table for them. In Europe, countries with a Roman Catholic heritage honor their dead with All Saints' Day and All Souls' Day. Mexico and much of Latin America have the Day of the Dead. All of these rituals to honor ancestors take place around the end of October and beginning of November, probably tied to the harvest time in the Northern Hemisphere.

Honoring ancestors is also widely practiced across the African continent. From Senegal to Madagascar, there are strongly held beliefs that worshipping and making offerings to ancestors can smooth things over in your present life. Traditions honoring ancestors are also practiced extensively in the Far East. In China, the Qingming Festival is celebrated on the 104th day after the winter solstice. People sweep the tombs of their ancestors, pray before them, and offer food and tea, among other things. In Japan and other Asian cultures, people return to their ancestral family spaces, clean their graves, and offer food, fruit, and wine. In Korea, these memorial services often go back to honor several generations of ancestors. In India, there are two periods of the year reserved for honoring ancestors: one in the spring and the other in the fall. Thailand has traditional dances to celebrate and honor the ties that link members of the clan to their ancestors where families visit the cemeteries and graves of their relatives, honoring them with candles and flowers.

The connection with our ancestors seems integral to almost every culture in the world—although the significance of these traditions often is lost through modernization. Also, almost all of these traditions are connected to rituals of prayer and food. The offering of food or drink appears to be linked to our connection to the earth that sustains us since, in the absence of food, you can no longer exist. Prayer can be seen as a linking mechanism that connects and raises the energetic vibrations of those who have passed on as well as those who have been left behind. Prayer links you to the invisible.

As the traditions across different countries suggest, you can honor your ancestors in many ways: visiting their graves, lighting a candle in their memory, or feeding others. Some traditions also suggest creating an ancestral altar to provide protective supportive energies in your space and to honor your lineage.

Alberto Villoldo, Ph.D., a Cuban-born psychologist, medical anthropologist, author, and shaman, believes that an ancestral altar can help you shed ancestral and karmic burdens. In his book, *The Four Insights: Wisdom, Power, and Grace of the Earthkeepers*, he writes that ancestral altars found in traditional cultures were used to prevent ancestors from "running amok in your house"—influencing you in ways you might not be aware of. "It's better to know where [the ancestors] are," he writes, "than to ignore their legacy."

In other words, *if there is no altar, you become the altar.*

So, honoring your ancestors helps you shift the transgenerational burden you carry. Aiding the spirits of those who have passed is both for them and for you. They move to higher frequencies and become more helpful to you so you can transform transgenerational burdens into ancestral blessings.

I have come to realize that altars are where negative energies get discharged, where people can let go of sadness, grief, anger, and other emotions. Altars also offer hope, protection, peace, and calm for the individual or family, becoming a place to express gratitude for life's special moments—a way to create a daily ritual for inviting the sacred into our life. It is also a ritual tool for inviting protective, supportive, uplifting energies into the home. Almost every home in India has some kind of altar. An altar creates a sacred frequency in our living space.

Most people will light a candle or tealight, burn incense, and put fresh flowers at the altar in the morning and evening. Incense or essential oils such as frankincense, sandalwood, and palo santo raise the frequency of your altar as these carry the vibrations of spiritual awakening, release material attachments, uplift, and expand while shielding the body and soul from negative influences. Candles represent fire, which by nature is a transformative element. Flowers absorb negative energies as does the offering of water. Sounds of crystal or singing bowls, chants, and other music also raise the vibrational frequency of the altar. I once lit a candle and placed a few drops of Angel's Trumpet flower essence—a transformative essence—on my altar to honor and help a soul journey on.

I stop at my home altar to connect with a feeling of gratitude or to become aware of my ancestors' influence on my life. It's a way of shifting how family history lives within us. Daniel Foor, author of *Ancestral Medicine: Rituals for Personal and Family Healing,* points out that when you speak well of your ancestors and offer heartfelt offerings through food, drink, and flowers, they receive the pleasure of remembrance and nourishment. In my personal experience, there's a relaxation of tension as unconscious patterns loosen and let go. We become more ready to heal any long-standing transgenerational challenges. that may have perpetuated these patterns. Working with our ancestors makes our lives and our relationships richer, rewarding, and deeply fulfilling.

## How to Set Up an Ancestral Altar

An ancestral altar like the ones Villoldo describes can be simple or elaborate. It can be as basic as a photograph flanked by the varied Hindu deities in a tarpaulin-covered fruit seller's makeshift stall. Or it can be an elaborate table with offerings of the traditional tobacco, glasses filled with water, aromatic incense, and fresh fruit surrounded by representations of the ancestors in the West African tradition. Whatever the format, the intention behind its creation is the most important element.

If you'd like to set up your own ancestral altar, choose a spot that's not in your bedroom. The altar is a place for discharging or attracting certain energies, so it is better to keep your ancestral altar out of your sleeping quarters. Only keep images of you, your partner, and your children in the bedroom. Energetically, photographs of parents and ancestors are better placed in a living room or family room. A raised surface like a shelf, a windowsill, or small table can be used to create an altar by putting down a piece of cloth and arranging photographs or symbols of your ancestors on it. You can use a fabric that might represent something from your culture or tradition, or any fabric that appeals to you. The root chakra, which represents our energetic connection to family at the base of the spine, is symbolized by the color red. So, if you wish, you can choose a fabric in this color to cover the surface.

You have a great degree of freedom to create how you would like to honor your ancestors. You might put photographs of your ancestors or objects that represent your lineage on or around the altar, such as an antique map that represents the part of the world your ancestry originated, an antique brooch, etc. If you have none of these kinds of objects, then, as Villoldo suggests, you can simply bring in representations from nature. He suggests putting out seasonal earth offerings such as shells in the summer or pine cones in the fall.

Ancestral healing work that involves working with the energies of our ancestors can be challenging. In India, the priests who perform the rituals for departed ancestors during the fortnight of ancestor veneration ground themselves and their space with protective prayers and sacred elements so that they can do this work. I, too, like to anchor the vibrational energy of an altar. You can do this with sacred objects that represent higher energies such as the Virgin Mary, Jesus, Buddha, Archangels, Kwan Yin, Ganesh, saints, or anything else you might be drawn to. If you would prefer, you can also use an abstract representation of the universal Spirit of Consciousness such as a painting, stone, or even a saying. While there is a great deal of freedom to create what appeals to you, you should anchor the altar with higher energies to provide you with protection.

And finally, include the five elements if you can: earth, fire, air, water, and sound. Crystals or flowers can represent earth, candles can represent fire, and incense or diffusion of essential oils can add the element of air. I've observed that altars in India often include a specific offering of water as well. The element of sound could be added through a bell, singing bowl, cymbals, etc. Elements need tending, so try and make sure that your altar doesn't become a spot for a collection of debris, old matches, incense ashes, or dust. Keep your altar clean and beautiful so that it nourishes you on your journey.

Once your altar is set up, you can visit it as a daily ritual. The more the altar appeals to your senses, the more likely you are to stop at it to light the candle or tealight, replace the flowers, and feel a sense of gratitude or reverence for your ancestors, your heritage, and your story—and not just see it as a piece of decor in your environment. As you work with your altar, you might get an insight or an answer to a question. Over time, the objects that you work with on your altar might also change as things shift in your own life; you may add or remove representations that you have placed there.

Once you start to interact with your altar and the objects on it, you start to change the way *your past lives within you.* "Working with this ancestral altar, you can change your family story at the mythic level," Villoldo says in *The Four Insights,* "where tales are epic journeys, not the same old tired sagas of emotional or material success or failure."

My client Phil lost his father when he was still in his early teens. His mother had remarried, and he was struggling in his relationship with her and her new husband, as well as with his own children and his ex-wife. I gave him a few flower essences and suggested that he light a candle before his father's photograph every night. If he wished, he could use this time to talk with his father and connect with him. Months later, when I saw Phil again, I could not believe the change. He looked younger—stress was no longer visible in his face—and he seemed calm, centered, and happy! He told me that he had felt propelled to make a series of changes in his life that he was previously unable to make. He had simplified his life, taking a less intense job, which freed up time for mountain biking. I strongly suspected that along with the essences, it was a result of the power of connecting to his father with love and gratitude. The creation of an altar *can* have a dramatic impact on our life.

Another client, Maureen, lit a candle for her close friend who had died of an incurable disease while he was still in his twenties. His passing had left a big hole in her life. As she looked at a framed photo of the two of them in happier days and let the candle beside it burn, Maureen meditated on what a good friend this man was. She did this for a few minutes each day. Sometimes, she would cry. Sometimes, she would laugh or simply let her love for him arise in her heart. A few months later, out of the blue, her friend's brother texted her. He'd been thinking of his brother and how close he had been to Maureen. Today, Maureen and her friend's brother have developed a romantic relationship with one another.

This is the power of working with our family energy field.

Working with the ancestral field varies across different traditions. In some cultural and spiritual traditions, you are trying to connect with ancestors who might be able to help you and guide you. These are often referred to as "well" or evolved ancestors, as opposed to those whose energies are trapped closer to the earth plane. In the Indian tradition, you are not looking to engage with your ancestors such as through dreamwork, or mediumship as in some other traditions, although you may receive messages or dreams from your ancestors. You are actively focused on gratitude and praying for their spiritual evolution so that their energies are not surrounding and affecting you. There are no specific ancestral altars, although ancestral photographs might be placed alongside other deities in a regular altar.

## The Power of Prayer

When you honor your ancestors, you allow them to continue their spiritual evolution. You stop living out their feelings, thoughts, frustrations, and desires. They become more helpful and powerful, guiding and helping you—their living descendants. When you pray for them, you support their spiritual evolution. In turn, they help you repair your troubled relationships and support you as part of their own journey of healing. You are able to create mutually supportive relationships even though you are separated by time.

It took years for me to find the words to explain why honoring our ancestors provides healing. It came to me when I reached into my tradition of Indian masters, who teach us the concepts of linear and non-linear time. Our physical bodies are moving in linear time, but our souls exist in non-linear time. Past, present, and future are simply constructs of the human mind. If you believe this, as I do, then it makes sense that our souls are connected to and carry information of the collective human field and can access the past—and the future. Emotions, since they are timeless and universal, can be seen as a linking mechanism that connects you to the energy of your ancestors and the invisible world.

## Prayers to Release the Past

There is a special fortnight in India in which you honor and pray for your ancestors. This time corresponds to the waning moon

from a full moon to the new moon. Different days of the fortnight are devoted to different members of the family lineages,
including honoring those who might have been killed in war,
through accidents or other forms of violence, or suicide. There
are even days to remember children who have died. Each day
of this period invites a particular blessing from the ancestors.
Finally, the last day is devoted to all the ancestors in the lineage
who have died. These traditions are accompanied by donations
of food and clothing to the priests who do the work during the
period and to those in need. Families often take that last day off
to visit the temple to pray for all their ancestors, or the priest
comes home to perform the ritual prayers. Thousands of people perform this ritual by the river—which is an incredible sight
to see.

Perhaps my ancestors wanted me to learn family constellations, because it was through constellations that I saw the
issues that many people faced were the result of ancestral issues
that went back in time several generations. It struck me that if
this ancestral energy was always hanging around, there was a
rationale for the traditions in my country to honor ancestors.
Ancestral burdens or blessings even showed up in horoscopes.
But, as I started to notice transgenerational family patterns that
repeated, it struck me that a form of protection would be simply
to offer prayers for the well-being of our ancestors.

Working with my clients and noticing karmic patterns, I
became aware of the importance of honoring my ancestors.
Since I didn't have access to priests or knowledge of the rituals, I
had to devise my own way to do this. I saw how family constellations invoked healing energies of love and compassion, so perhaps that was the way. I created a ritual based on my experiences
with my clients and the intention behind these rituals—which is

honoring, acknowledging, and remembering. If ancestral energy was hanging around us all the time, why wait for an annual ritual; why not do it daily? The word *tarpanam* means offering. So, I created a short prayer, or *tarpanam*, for my ancestors and did it every day. *Tarpanam* is not just an act of service for your ancestors; it is also the greatest gift you can give yourself. By remembering and honoring my ancestors, their sacrifices, and challenges, I became aware of the wisdom of my personal history. That is when I started to notice shifts showing up in my connections with my family. Cousins called me, photographs of my grandparents and other relatives showed up, connections started to strengthen and appear. Healing was happening. The most profound shift after doing this ritual for my ancestors was a sense of peace. I started to feel deeply connected to my ancestral lineages, to have compassion for their stories and an appreciation for the ones I knew personally. Slowly, this ritual has taken on deeper meaning and significance in my life.

## Your Ancestors Want to Connect with You Too

Shifts in the invisible world with my ancestors began to manifest in the visible world—and it all happened after I started doing *tarpanam*. Several years ago, I arrived in India in the early hours of the morning after a twenty-four-hour flight from the US. A relative of mine who I hadn't seen for several decades came to see me that morning and woke me from my jet-lag-induced slumber. I had just arrived in India, and she was visiting from another city; we were overlapping only by a day. After some perfunctory greetings, she immediately dove into stories of my paternal grandmother and my father's childhood that I had never heard before. I heard stories about a great-aunt, tough on everyone, but who indulged my father as the youngest child. I felt as if the ancestors just couldn't wait to talk with me!

I knew little of my paternal grandmother's life, and with my father and his siblings gone, I yearned to know more about her. A few months later, back in the US, I unexpectedly received a photograph of my paternal grandparents from a cousin: she'd found it in her family archives. Up until then, I didn't have a photograph of them. More information about my ancestors, in the form of stories or photographs, came from family members. Because of this, I've connected with cousins that I had lost touch with or even never met. In the last few years, my relationships with my father's family have grown deeper and my ability to share my journey and insights with my cousins has grown.

I also noticed something else: after I started the daily practice of *tarpanam*, I felt much more at peace. With it came a sense of connection, gratitude, wisdom, insight, and of being *held*. I could feel the deep love of my ancestors and the strength of both my lineages standing behind me. I started to feel supported in my life, part of a larger whole, with a growing sense of trust that the Universe was there to guide me. I would sometimes see an image of a net being repaired: thick rope closing holes until it could hold us all.

These experiences or synchronicities are not mine alone. Many people who start the practice of honoring their ancestors notice new connections in their lives as they experience the collective force that supports all of us. I have, over the years, encouraged many of my clients to practice *tarpanam* to heal strained relationships and shift family patterns. They usually see an improvement in relationships with their parents and extended family and, like me, they also experience a greater sense of peace. As communication improves, loving and supporting relationships develop even between those in conflict. My clients report receiving calls from estranged family members, or family mementos suddenly show up as if to signal healing of a family member who has passed.

In return for honoring them, your ancestors will bless you since you represent a part of them still in the physical realm. They will support you from their world and help you to establish healthy boundaries, forgive the past and those who have hurt you, and show up in more conscious ways with your living family. To me, it is the most powerful ritual a person can do on a daily basis.

## How to Do Tarpanam

Here is a modified daily practice of *tarpanam*. It only takes a few minutes, but the effects are profound. The more grateful I was for my ancestors, the more gratitude I experienced for the journey of my life and the challenges I faced, as I could see my life story as part of a larger tapestry.

Imagine yourself standing before your ancestors. Your maternal ancestors to your right and your paternal ancestors to the left. They extend before you almost like the V shape made by the pattern of flying geese. Each ancestor has two ancestors behind them.

If you wish, you may fold your hands and bow before the two lineages before you.

This is the prayer that I say to each of my lineages, and you may wish to adapt it for yourself or choose words that resonate with you. It can be done between sunrise and sunset. I do it once in the morning.

*To my maternal lineage, three generations before me, I bow before you. May the lineage be in peace and love and light and harmony. May each of you be in peace, love, light, and harmony. I am grateful for all that I have received from this lineage, including the gifts of the challenges I face.*

*To my paternal lineage, three generations before me, I bow before you. May the lineage be in peace and love and light and harmony. May each of you be in peace, love, light, and harmony. I am grateful for all that I have received from this lineage, including the gifts of the challenges I face.*

As I say it, I'm very conscious of my breathing, which grounds me and helps me enter a state of gratitude.

I now visualize the current living generations standing in front of this lineage: the children (mine and my nieces and nephews) in front, my generation standing behind them, those in my parents' generation behind us. Three generations in front of the ancestral lineages.

The prayer goes like this—or at least this is my adaptation of it:

*From this place of light, love, and harmony, I ask you to bless us as we all stand here before you.*

*I ask you to bless all the children in the lineage, including those who are yet to come.*

*I ask you to bless all of us who stand behind these children as we struggle and muddle through. Bless us with your love and guidance. May there always be peace and harmony among us.*

*I ask you to bless those who stand behind us, including those who I may not know or may have forgotten.*

*Om, Shanthi, Shanthi, Shanthi.*
(Translated: *peace, peace, peace.*)

I say the prayer for my entire clan—maternal and paternal—even though I don't know everyone in either family. If I am angry with someone, I try to release those feelings and ask for support from the maternal or paternal lineage to heal the relationships. If someone I know needs to be particularly taken care of, I can ask for specific help. Over time, as you get comfortable, you can adapt the prayer to honor six generations of ancestors who have passed on.

You are free to adapt it in any way that calls to you. The only thing you don't want to ask for is the soul to "rest" in peace—because the soul is on a journey. If you have a practice from your tradition that you are familiar with, I encourage you to do that instead.

Even if you don't want to do *tarpanam*, just as in traditions all over the world, you can serve the poor, children, the elderly, and others who need it. You can also honor your ancestors by giving back to society what you received from them—money, education, or taking care of those in need. Acts of charity and feeding others are, in fact, universal ways to honor others across the world. You can also serve the earth consciously and embrace a spirit of reverence for nature. These acts connect our soul with our ancestors and are a way of honoring our roots that nurture us.

# PART III

# Understanding Your Family Energy Field

# — SEVEN —

# Rewriting Your Parental Story

O ne day, I came home from work to find that a large tree had fallen, blocking the road. I knew that tree. It provided shelter from the summer sun. It was always there, a welcome sight when I drove down my street. Now it lay on its side, roots exposed. For a tree of that size, the roots seemed quite shallow. When the crew came to cut the tree up, I spoke to the arborist about this.

He told me it was because the tree grew at the edge of the sidewalk, surrounded by concrete. "It's not able to penetrate deeply enough," he said, "so all it had were shallow roots."

I went into my house, thinking about that. Deep roots nourish and sustain us in the face of storms and challenges in life. Otherwise, you live shallowly, and any success can be temporary, even brittle, and failure debilitating. Nourishment comes to me from the work I've done with my ancestral energy fields and the support I receive from the flower essences. This work does not release me from facing the storms of life but does give me support to face them. For your ancestors too, whether your parents or those that came before them, trauma or challenges were inevitable. At the most fundamental level, parents give you the greatest gift you can receive: your life. Consequently, your parents are your most immediate roots. When you experience challenges in your life and relationships and struggle to deal with them, how do you start to feel grateful for the gift of life? You are the blossom of your family tree. How do you find the capacity to blossom?

Whether or not you feel your parents' love and continue to receive it as you get older, the reality is that parents give life and children receive it, and this creates a structure of loyalty that is both conscious and unconscious. Parents feel entitled to their expectations, and children feel obligated to fulfill these expectations. Children too have expectations of love and acceptance, which may sometimes feel completely out of reach. The entitlements and obligations of these relationships might be obvious to you because of conversations and interactions you've had with your parents, or they might be hidden from your awareness, yet strongly influencing you, nonetheless.

## The Debt of Life: Parents Give and Children Receive

Quite often, at the heart of conflicted relationships with our parents is the violation of this rule that underlies the family energy field—"parents give and children receive." There is a specific word in Sanskrit for the debt you owe your parents: *matr rin*, and *pitr rin*, where *rin* means debt, *matr* is mother, and *pitr* is father.

By acknowledging the preciousness of a human birth, which can only be achieved through your parents, this principle of the family energy field recognizes the debt that you "owe" your parents, independent of their behavior and personality.

At some level, we all want to have happy, loving families and relationships. And maybe you feel that to a large extent you do. On the other hand, if your relationships are less than nourishing, or you find it hard to say no, or struggle with intimacy or commitment, you might want to look at your parental relationships. It's very difficult to have the relationships that you desire if you don't resolve your relationships with your parents. They lay the blueprint for our experience of all others. When you have a warm, affectionate relationship with your parents, you feel secure in yourself. You see others as trustworthy without knowing if that will indeed be the case. In intimate relationships, you can maintain a balance between dependence and independence. But for some, there may be very basic violations in this relationship.

You can be hurt by the inattention of your parents, their inability to express their love, their criticism of you because of their expectations, their coldness, or their treatment of you. The list of ways in which they might hurt you, even if they're trying their best not to, is endless. When you are triggered by their behaviors, you might resolve to do things differently, but you get pushed into your automatic response patterns, and your resolve is hopelessly lost. You may feel as if you are sometimes spinning your wheels in a drama that repeats itself again and again. You may be stuck because of the stories you have always been told or even the ones you tell yourself. To release these stories, we need to see how trauma affects our roots.

## How Trauma Affects Your Roots

For most of us, our family history has been shaped by the tectonic movements of war, victimization, poverty, hunger, suicide, and other powerful forces, just as the earth has been shaped by the movement of glaciers, earthquakes, volcanoes, and other forces of nature. Your family canvas is vast, and you are but a brushstroke on this painting. To see it all is overwhelming. To really see how it might have shaped you is probably beyond the scale of your human consciousness. However, sometimes, you are able to see a narrow slice of your history through the viewfinder of constellations or other energy work.

Trauma of any kind is inevitable and is part of the experience of being human. You cannot completely protect yourself or your children from having stressful or shocking experiences. These can cause an inability to express love, to parent, to relate to others with warmth, acceptance, and intimacy. They can even prevent a person from being able to earn a living. Your experience and perception of trauma give rise to emotions such as fear, anger, sadness, grief, or powerlessness.

What do I mean by trauma? While there can be an injury to the physical body, the psychological impact of trauma is a response to stress that becomes automatic whenever you are reminded of the original wounding. Your response can be conscious, but most often, it's subconscious. Neuroscience suggests that the conscious mind "runs the show" only about 5 percent of the time. The other 95 percent of the time, you are operating from the ingrained and inherited programs of your subconscious mind—completely unaware of it.

Trauma is an unprocessed story—whether it's middle school bullying, the trials of immigration, heartbreak, war, and many other incidents that leave us wounded. The trauma that you experience affects different people in different ways. One person can recover from heartbreak while another might completely withdraw. Someone laid off from their job might try to find ways of pursuing their passion while another person may completely give up. When you are overwhelmed by a traumatic experience, you can't intellectually or emotionally process what has happened. Understanding the experience within the larger context of life is not possible at that time. Instead, you might experience a deep sense of despair, of being alienated from others, a loss of faith, of not belonging to your family or a larger network that could support you. Your connection to yourself and to others is ruptured. You may develop unhealthy patterns of behavior to help you cope.

The late Ivan Boszormenyi-Nagy, a therapist who worked with thousands of families across different socioeconomic backgrounds, observed that people who have been wronged, abused, or hurt, and cannot get amends from the people who have hurt them, may end up ill-treating others. Because of their own experience, they try to get retribution by harming others who are not responsible for wounding them. This perpetuates a cycle of trauma, abuse, or wounding, eroding trust in relationships. Boszormenyi-Nagy, in his book *Invisible Loyalties*, called this behavior "destructive entitlement." Visible symptoms of destructive entitlement include the absence of remorse, child and partner abuse, and even prejudice toward others including racial or religious persecution.

Is it possible to connect to the roots of your existence if it runs through your parents, who have betrayed your trust? Can you reframe or recalibrate your relationship so that it doesn't cast a shadow on your life? To access the gift of life, you have to start letting go of the parental stories you have believed and held so tightly; you have to stop *carrying* your parents through these stories. Just as Christine, in the constellation described in Chapter 4, was able to have compassion for her mother by seeing her as someone else's child, and then understanding the effects that trauma had on her grandmother, perhaps you too can start to reframe your parents', grandparents', and ancestors' experiences. For instance, you might say to yourself:

> *I have felt unloved. However, I now know that my mother was too depressed to express her love to me. I believe that even if I didn't feel it, she loved me. It's okay for me to feel sad or angry about her lack of loving behavior toward me. I'm thankful for her gift of life to me. I'm thankful that because she didn't express love, I have learned how important it is to be kind and nurturing to your children, to hug them and say, "I love you." I'm grateful for the lessons I have learned because they make me the parent I am today.*

> *I have felt unworthy, but I now believe that everyone, including me, is worthy of happiness in this life. It's okay for me to slip back into feeling unworthy of happiness, but when that happens, I choose to be loving toward myself. I remember that while my parents were always very critical of me, they gave me life. They wouldn't criticize me if they didn't care. But I also understand that their need to criticize me has more to do with what is going on inside them than any choices I'm making or how I live my life. I do not have to take in their criticism.*

Dysfunctional family patterns such as shutting down or engaging in passive-aggressive behavior or other coping mechanisms are created over time as a family tries to deal with stress and trauma. When you begin to look at the role of trauma in your family, you begin the journey to healing any parental wounds within you. You can also let go of the ceiling on what you can accomplish, and on perceiving the joy and wonder of life. You can experience the warmth of relationships and find the strength to go after your dreams. You can step forward into a life you will have created for yourself, letting go of the suffering you've been holding on to so you can start to see that your life is indeed a gift.

For people who have been physically, emotionally, or sexually abused by their parents, or hurt in other ways, the process of accepting the gift of life can be extremely challenging. Letting go of the suffering if your parents have been abusive requires more support than this book is able to provide. For these readers, I would strongly recommend including other resources such as a therapist in your journey to heal your roots. Since I am not a professionally trained therapist, most of my advice here is for those whose parents were not abusive. However, I have observed that family constellation therapy can be quite helpful in such cases if you can find a skilled facilitator, and there are certain flower essences and exercises that are listed in this book that can also give some relief. Even if it's impossible to accept your parents, you can heal the parental wound within you and feel the gift of life. You can tap into the roots of the tree of life, rather than be overwhelmed by the shadow that darkens your life. You do not have to engage with your parents, and for some, they may not be physically alive or emotionally available, but you can release some of the pain of this negative energy.

## Understanding Your Parental Wounds

Self-worth, inherent within us at a soul level, can be eroded by our childhood or other experiences. As a child, you are constantly absorbing messages about yourself from interactions around you. Millions of experiences, significant and minuscule, create these self-beliefs. In particular, your mother's reactions to you as a child strongly influence how you perceive yourself. Her patience or impatience, her ability or inability to express warmth, love, and tenderness, her sadness and her joy—all her emotions—shape your personality, especially up to the preteen years and often into adulthood.

In the late 1980s, Michael J. Meaney, Ph.D., and his research team at McGill University began examining the relationships among stress, maternal care, and gene expression. These researchers looked at the long-term effects of separating rodent mothers from their newborn pups for several minutes each day and found that the adult pups were more prone to stress and showed changes in certain regions of their brain. However, the behavior of the mother on being reunited with her pups— namely the extent to which she licked and groomed her pups— was important. The mother's rate of grooming affected the pups' future stress response. More grooming led to a more modest stress response. Less grooming led to the pups later being more fearful—changes that persisted over two generations! Through this experiment, we can see responses to trauma vary and can have long-term effects. And trauma for a newborn or preverbal child can simply be separation from the mother or father or both for a relatively short period of time.

Separation from your parents when young can lead to a parenting wound—a loss of trust that your parents will be there for you in life. Your parents may have loved you dearly but inadvertently caused this wound. Maybe your mother was hospitalized when you were young, causing a separation, or your father lost his job and became depressed and withdrawn before he was able to get a new position and return to being the stable father figure he had been before. Maybe a new sibling was born, or you had so many siblings that your mother wasn't able to give you the attention you needed. Perhaps one of your parents died when you were a child, or you experienced their absence due to divorce, incarceration, or working far away from home for a long stretch of time. All these events can cause a wound without the parent having any idea that it is happening. In response to the wound, you might have pulled away emotionally from the parent and unconsciously decided that people who love you can't be trusted to stick around, internalizing the deeply harmful message that "I must be unlovable." If the other parent is around, it can mitigate the wounding, but it may not prevent it completely.

John Bowlby, a psychoanalyst who studied children that had been orphaned by World War II in England, was the first to provide evidence of the impact of the loss of mothering or parenting. Children who had been separated from their mothers early in their lives for a prolonged period of time failed to thrive in society and live ethical lives. Many of them even became thieves. Martin Seligman, in his book *Authentic Happiness*, quotes Bowlby as describing these children as "affectionless, lacking feeling, with only superficial relationships, angry, and anti-social." Many of the children in his study also had fathers who were either absent completely, had deserted the family, or were hostile or violent toward their children. This led him to claim that a strong parent–child bond is irreplaceable.

To examine his theory, Bowlby observed sick children in a hospital and watched what happened when their parents came to visit. In those days, parents were allowed to visit their children only once a week for an hour. He found that children went through three stages. At first, they would protest strongly when their parents left: they would cry, scream, pound the door, rattle the crib for a few hours or even days. In the second stage, after the parents left, the children experienced despair: they would whimper or become listless. And finally, they would "detach." They became sociable with other adults and kids and accepted a new caregiver but expressed detachment from their parents by showing no joy when they returned. His findings showed how dependent children are on attention from their parents, and the type of emotional damage that can occur when there is a lapse.

Once, in a meditation class, the instructor asked each person to meditate and go within. "Ask yourself, what is your deepest fear? When something comes up, hold it, and then go back within. Ask yourself, what is your deepest fear? If it's the same fear repeatedly, then you know you have reached your deepest fear. If not, go deeper." There are only closely related core wounds, I heard her say: that we are not "worthy" or that we are "unlovable." Underlying these wounds is fear of rejection and abandonment and the need to fit in with the "tribe" to survive.

How does a child make sense of feeling unloved or unworthy? While you might not articulate an explanation even as an adult, deep within us, we might feel:

> *I'll never be loved for who I am.*

> *I'm a fool for thinking I can achieve my heart's desire.*

> *Yes, I'm unhappy, but I don't deserve any better than what I have right now.*

How you experience your relationships with your parents very early on can cause you to feel unloved and unworthy. Mark Wolynn, author of *It Didn't Start with You*, points out that if mothers are "attuned" to their children even 20 to 30 percent of the time, that's "good enough" mothering. Your mother didn't have to be perfect for you to feel loved. Even what seems like a little is actually enough.

But if there's no connection at all or if they are not emo tionally responsive, you start to feel something's wrong with *you*. An unarticulated belief about yourself gets entrenched in your mind, and pain lodges in your heart. You start to see yourself as not worthy of receiving love unless you have earned it in some way—that you are unlovable as you are. You may even feel a sense of shame or embarrassment inside you that's also perhaps not fully articulated.

## Rewriting Your Parental Story

When you shift your relationships with your parents within yourself, you allow yourself to feel worthy of connection with others. You heal your core wound of unworthiness.

When Sara came to see me, her father had died, and she didn't get along with her mother. Every time she went to see her mom, they fought. Sara would leave planning never to talk to her or see her mother again. I gave Sara flower essences to heal the emotional grief and release some of the bitterness she carried. I also wanted Sara to explore some of the history of her maternal lineage for deeper healing.

I learned that Sara's mother was adopted by a couple who had no other children. The adoptive mother was very strict and never showed Sara's mother any affection. When it came to discipline and expectations, she was tough. The adoptive father was an alcoholic and when he was in a rage, he was abusive to Sara's mother and threatened to take her back to the orphanage. Sara's mother never wanted to know her biological parents.

As we worked through the story of her lineage and the repetition of emotional patterns, it became possible for Sara to see her mother differently. She realized that given the stories her mother had told her, her mother had never received much affection, so she could not be demonstrative to her children. When her mother was abusive to Sara and threw her out of the house, telling her not to come back, she was just repeating what had been done to her. Sara was part of a story that stretched back in time.

Whose anger are we experiencing? Underneath that rage, whose grief is it? Once you start to recognize that someone else has projected their anger and grief onto you—perhaps through their own experiences, or these emotions might even be encoded into the family energy field—then you can start to reclaim your personal power. Awareness is the first step, and it can provide you with the freedom to make conscious choices. Once you become aware of the patterns at play, you can choose to break the cycle of destructive entitlement, and your expectations of both your parents and of yourself. You can start to heal your parental wounds.

When you shift, longed-for changes in your relationships and in other areas of your life might not happen right away. You might imagine in your mind's eye that you have a closer, less painful relationship with your parents. Elated and hopeful, you might find that your expectations come up against the reality of where your parents, partners, or others really are. They might snap back at you or criticize you as they are accustomed to doing. This can feel discouraging as subconsciously, you might be seeking outer validation of your inner changes. When you continue getting rankled, it simply means that there is more work to be done, though this is internal work. Eventually, the more you shift, the more things will shift around you, as the Universe synchronizes with the change in your attitude. Ultimately, it is important that you shift your responses and release the effect of the negative patterns on you.

In order for you to be successful, you do need to be patient, and you can use flower essences, ancestral altars, and prayers to support you in making these changes.

## Releasing Your Unconscious Loyalty to Your Parents

When you view yourself as a victim, you may pull away emotionally from your parents and find it challenging to accept them as they are. But by remaining in the role of a victim, you violate the rules of the family energy field, which in turn then affects you negatively—keeping you locked in repeating patterns. In your desire for love, acceptance, acknowledgment, or any other expectation from your parents, you remain *unconsciously* loyal— even if you have nothing to do with them and believe they no longer have any influence on you.

When you are unconsciously loyal, you might repeat the very behaviors your parents exhibited, the behaviors that caused so much pain. To identify unconscious loyalties that can be getting in the way of a client's happiness and well-being, I search for the clues that show me the negative family patterns they might not recognize. These patterns hint at an unconscious desire to be connected to a parent in a way that might be unhealthy and even destructive.

Here are some instances from my practice:

- Kate's father abused her, and she hates him for it. But in her family, she is the only child who has the same autoimmune disorder he had.

- Brad distanced himself from his alcoholic father, disparaging him, but now drinks to excess himself.
- Sean was having an affair with a married woman, and she became pregnant. He ended up marrying her though he hadn't intended to, just as his father married his own pregnant girlfriend (the woman who became Sean's mother) out of a sense of obligation. Sean did not have a good relationship with his father and repeated his father's pattern, despite being aware of his father's dissatisfaction with his own decision.
- Ed's father was a prominent lawyer and had a successful practice but was an alcoholic, had affairs, and ultimately went bankrupt. Ed too did not have a good relationship with his father, and he started an affair at about the same age as his father had as well. His law practice started to deteriorate, leading to his second divorce.
- Liz, a successful businesswoman, constantly criticized her husband because of his inability to hold down a job. She had to shoulder the responsibility of financial security for her family. Her daughter ended up in a marriage where she too took on the responsibility of being the primary earner. Liz's son hasn't married; he drifts from one job to another.
- Max's father was overlooked for promotion repeatedly, keeping him stuck in a low-level managerial position. The same pattern appeared in Max's life as a ceiling on his professional life, despite his best efforts to move up the corporate ladder.

While these examples have clear parallels between generations, some negative unconscious patterns in relationships may only be visible when you look closely. When I work with clients, I see how the burden of expectations can make us feel as if we are coming apart at the seams. A person might insist that they will never be anything like their parents, and yet they could end up mirroring their behavior in specific ways. In the last example, Liz's daughter mirrored her mother's behavior, but she might have ended up being more like her brother, unfocused and not persevering at a career, which would be following the pattern of her father. What I see is a family pattern playing out a bit differently in the second generation than in the first. But looking closely may reveal an unconscious loyalty to your parents and the repetition of family patterns.

The very gift of life—for which you are indebted—makes you unconsciously loyal to your ancestral energy field and to your parents, even if you do not feel grateful for it. Even if your relationship with your parents is strained, even if you hold back affection from them or avoid them entirely, you may still be unconsciously loyal—so much so that you may be willing to sacrifice your own happiness for them, without even realizing what you are doing.

You arrive into this world entangled in the story, or karma, of your family. Indian masters say that there are many souls waiting to be born on this earth, waiting for the right family where lessons can be learned, and the right alignment of planets, so that these souls can fulfill their destinies. Family is the crucible through which you work through your individual and family karma. This philosophy embraces the point of view that your life is not a random event, and you are not just the outcome of a sperm successfully chasing an egg. The challenges your parents present you with shape you into what you become. It's as if there is a family contract you agreed to before being born, and your arrival into the human experience opens a gateway for your soul to attempt to fulfill its purpose here on earth. Human love is an imperfect offering, tinged with expectation and judgment. Perhaps your soul unfettered from your body has wisdom that can release the ego from psychological bondage to step into freedom and empowerment.

Being grateful for your life does not mean that you sanction the behavior of your parents or their particular model of parenting. If you think of life as a river, your parents, by giving you life, allow you to be part of the flow forward. Even a client, Kate, who had been abused by her father, noticed that she had inherited his scientific mind. Another client, Lara, had inherited her mother's artistic talents. If you have associated a characteristic of yours with a parent who wounded you, you might deny those parts of yourself and never allow yourself to express them out in the world.

Choosing to see is choosing to be conscious. And it takes courage to see the unconscious patterns and behavior at play. Carl Jung said that until you make the unconscious conscious, it will direct your life and you will call it fate. Whether you distance yourself from your parents because of childhood experiences or as a result of patterns of dysfunctional behaviors in the family, closing yourself off can limit your potential for living life to the fullest. Many people are advised to cut off their parents to reduce the pain of their dynamic with them and to help them let go of hurtful memories. But cutting off from a parent physically or emotionally, in and of itself, doesn't heal the family energy field because this doesn't stop them from affecting your life energetically or stop family patterns from repeating. As Dan Cohen, author of *I Carry Your Heart in My Heart*, points out, "People who reject their parents may be fully justified in their assessment of fault and blame, but *unaware of the heavy consequences that often results from this attitude*." The question to ask, perhaps, is, What are you rejecting? Along with physical and emotional proximity, you might also be rejecting the possibility of freeing yourself from the parental story you hold.

To reject your parents is to remain tied to expectations of what you would have wanted from them and to remain a victim of fate or circumstance. To accept them is simply to accept the reality of who they are. It is not about forgetting what your parents might have done or that you justify, accept, or condone harmful actions or behavior. When you reject them, you are in effect struggling to come to terms with the reality and disappointment of your expectations. To accept them means realizing you may never get the acknowledgment of the hurt, disappointment, betrayal, grief, or any other emotions you feel as a result of their behavior. You may never get the appreciation and validation you want from them. It means accepting the reality of the parenting you received instead of being attached to the notion of who you would have liked them to be or what you would have liked them to do, in the past, present, or future. It might even mean that you realize that some of their actions, however hurtful, were governed by their own fears and pain, or by their desire for your well-being, no matter how misguided. It also means letting go of the need for revenge, the need to be right, and the need to blame your parents for your current circumstances. If possible, it means developing compassion and understanding for their journey and for them, even if you don't plan to ever be in contact with them or share these feelings with them. Accepting them is a letting go of victimhood. When you do this, you start to heal your family energy field and release the burden and the imprint of negative patterns. For some, this journey is more difficult than for others, and I urge those readers for whom this is incredibly challenging to find the outside support you need.

You can't get attached to seeing your parents change just because you have changed, but you can know that due to your healing work, your feelings will shift, and you will feel less vulnerable and powerless. You might even choose a spiritual perspective, accepting your parents' flaws as well as their strengths, and by doing so, reclaim your own power.

There may or may not be hope for improving your relationship with your parents, but one thing is for certain: you can heal the parental wound *within yourself*, freeing yourself from the pain of the past. By doing the inner work to value yourself, you have consciously rejected the idea that you're unworthy of love; you've committed to taking responsibility for your own choices and decisions. This detachment allows you to be less reactive and consciously shape your relationship with your parents and with yourself. It allows you to see other people's actions as a function of *themselves*, not as a reflection of *you*.

When you find your self-worth, you can set your boundaries and choose to relate to people differently. This protects you from getting hurt as you once were, mostly because you can see that it's not about you.

Would Sara someday be able to completely let go of her anger and her bitterness toward her mother? Maybe, maybe not. But I have confidence that a client like Sara will someday be able to arrive at a place where she can say, "My mother had a hard life, and that was a big part of why she behaved as she did. I can feel however I do about her treatment of me, but I recognize that she was not necessarily able to be different." She might even gain compassion for her mother's story and adopt this new story instead of the one she has held onto for so long so she can begin to set healthy boundaries. In fact, she has done so already. With the help of the flower essences, Sara created an optimal energetic distance that allowed her to have a relationship with her mother *and* take care of herself. She might even become a healer within her family—modeling to others new ways of relating to those within the family who caused them pain.

Unresolved traumas can overwhelm families, communities, and even countries for generations and keep getting passed down to each subsequent generation. As you continue to shift, you become less emotionally reactive. You start to see these behaviors for what they are—ways of coping with pain. And you can stop taking them personally because you can see they didn't originate with you.

Starting the journey to healing your relationships, finding gratitude for your life and self-worth, starts with accepting your parents. In doing so, you learn to let go of your expectations of both them and of yourself. The way your parents behave may stay the same, even if you do the inner healing work for yourself. But because your perspective shifts, you create space in your heart for the relationship as it is, not as you would like it to be. You will still suffer hurt at times, but you will stop getting in your own way and reopening old wounds again and again. You can trust yourself to pick yourself up and grow in strength and wisdom.

## Connecting with Universal Unconditional Love

In family constellation therapy, I observed that if parenting had been inadequate, Emily and Dan often asked participants to represent healing maternal or paternal energies. These were archetypal energies and seemed to parallel the representations of divine healing energies I had observed while growing up. I realized that one of the ways you can heal is by accessing the loving, nurturing energy of the divine mother and father archetypes.

The divine mother archetype is one of the most ancient and exists in many spiritual narratives such as the Virgin Mary in Catholicism, Kwan Yin, the Buddhist Goddess of Compassion, and so many others. In Hinduism, there are many manifestations of the goddess, often personalized as a mother who takes many forms. She might be loving, forgiving, tender, fierce, or merciless in her discipline. There are temples scattered all over the country in honor of the divine feminine or the divine mother. Men and women will make a pilgrimage to these temples often because "the mother has called." While the divine mother rules the pantheon of deities, her consort invokes the archetypal divine male energy. The most popular hymn and chant in India promotes the idea that these divine energies alone are the quintessential mother and father.

It may be harder to imagine a divine father energy that is not authoritarian or disciplinarian, but perhaps you can imagine a protective, nurturing, compassionate energy that resonates with your spiritual leanings such as Jesus, Buddha, a Universal Father, or some of the energies from the Hindu pantheon.

To repair your connection to your ancestors, you can start by opening a connection to being nurtured. The more you can access these energies and lean on them, the more you can fill the void within you and release your expectations of your human parents and other people around you. You can open yourself to receiving love, support, and guidance, building a connection from within, taking care of your own needs without resenting others for not doing so. The visualization exercise below can help you access these energies and shift the parental wounds within you.

Many well-known athletes use visualization to create detailed, vivid internal mental images of their performance before they actually perform. This process trains the brain by strengthening the mind–body connection through multiple cognitive processes, which in turn increases confidence, performance, and success. In addition to reducing stress, visualization allows you to shift your thoughts and behaviors because the subconscious doesn't recognize that it's not a real experience.

## Healing through Visualization

Stand in a comfortable position and take a few centering breaths with your eyes closed. Think of what you would like to invite into your life—a loving partnership, warm relationships with your children, or security and abundance. Imagine the divine universal mother standing behind you with her right hand on your left shoulder. Now imagine the divine universal father standing behind you with his left hand on your right shoulder. Breathe in their love, nurturance, and protection. Feel the gentleness of their hands and the support it gives you.

Can you imagine almost leaning back into them as they bear the weight of you? Feel them giving you permission to receive whatever it is that you wish for so deeply in your life. Feel their blessings for the fullness of your life coming into bloom. Feel their support for your success as they wish for you what you have trouble visualizing and asking for yourself. Feel their love for you. When you're ready, take a step forward with your right foot and then your left foot. Continue to feel their hands on your shoulders. Inhale, feel their love, and breathe it in, knowing that it is always there for you, that you can reach into it and tap into it anytime. Do this daily until you can truly feel this loving universal parenting energy and its support in your life.

## Journal Exercises

1. In the last chapter, we discussed the possible trauma that parents or grandparents may have experienced. In your story, for instance, your father might have gone to war or lost one of his parents. Your mother's family might have experienced hardship or violence in some form. Can you explore how these backstories shaped them into who they became? Did they have to leave or flee their country of birth? Was a parent or grandparent abandoned? Do you know any of the challenges your grandparents might have had to go through? I recommend using your altar and the flower essences listed below to help you work through these journaling questions and in managing the emotions that might come up.

2. Do you have any early memories of being left alone? Did your parents have to leave you with a grandparent or other relative? Were you hospitalized, or were either of your parents? Do you prefer to keep an emotional or physical distance from your parents? Is it possible for you to explore what incidents made you feel that way? If you were abused as a child, I would highly recommend including a therapist in this journal exercise.

## Flower Essences

**Chicory**—for releasing expectations that may be keeping you locked in unconscious patterns.

**Willow**—for bitterness against your parents, fate, or circumstances.

**Holly**—for anger at your parents, siblings, or other family members.

**Honeysuckle**—for releasing the memories of the past that prevent you from being in the present.

**Star of Bethlehem**—for soothing the grief within. It is often called a mothering essence.

**Sweet Chestnut**—for when the burden of expectations or the challenges you are dealing with leave you feeling like you are at the end of your rope or have reached the limits of your endurance.

**Mariposa Lily**—for healing wounds related to mothering.

**Baby Blue Eyes**—for healing parental wounds related to the father.

**Post-trauma Stabilizer**—a healing blend of essences to treat the symptoms of PTSD (see the Glossary for individual essences that make up this blend).

**Mustard**—for depression that seems to come on unexpectedly. It releases unconscious karmic experiences.

**Wild Rose**—for apathy and feeling resigned in life and lacking the incentive to make changes.

*See Glossary for details about these essences.*

# EIGHT

# Parents Give and You Receive

A s I discussed in the last chapter, one of the primary laws of the family energy field is that *parents give and children receive.* What happens when you are unable to receive your parents' love or if you give more than you receive? You struggle with boundaries and self-care. How does this happen?

Sam's girlfriend came for a consultation because she was frustrated with their relationship. I learned that Sam's father had died of a sudden heart attack when he was fourteen. In the weeks that followed, he watched his mother spiral downward from shock. She came home tired and exhausted from work and seemed lost and unresponsive to the sounds around her.

Sam had two younger siblings and when they played, his mother, who used to smile at them, make comments, and even sometimes join in their fun for a few minutes, began to ignore them completely. She was so preoccupied, in fact, that Sam often ended up making dinner for himself and his younger siblings.

As he grew older, Sam grew even more protective of his family. Although he left home and lived independently, he often took care of them financially. His first marriage failed even though everything seemed to start off smoothly. Now, in another long-term relationship, his girlfriend was bitter about his inability to commit and the priority his mother had in his life.

Without knowing it, Sam had stepped into the space that his father held in the family, financially and emotionally. In trying to unconsciously fill the vacuum left by his father, Sam took on a burden that overwhelmed him. For the sake of his relationship, Sam needed to put his relationship first, but having taken on the role of filling his father's shoes, he could not step out of it.

The ramifications of the first principle of the family energy field—*parents give and children receive*—are far-reaching. The giving between parents and children can never be equal because parents give life, which means they give more. When the roles are reversed and this principle is violated by children trying to "give" to their parents, it can lead to unhappiness for the child. Whether you realize it or not, trying to emotionally nurture your parents creates a barrier to opening yourself to deep connections and trusting in the flow of life.

## The Queen of Strengths

In a constellation workshop, I once heard a participant say, "It's almost easier to hurt someone than it is to be vulnerable and open yourself completely to being loved." It was a telling observation. Allowing ourselves to love completely and freely also makes us more vulnerable to getting hurt. To prevent that, we often barricade our hearts to feel secure. More than the capacity to love others, including parents, George Vaillant has called the capacity to receive love, or to be loved, the "Queen of Strengths." For thirty years, from 1972 to 2004, Vaillant, a psychiatrist and professor at Harvard Medical School, oversaw and directed a study that tracked the lives of 268 Harvard University sopho-mores from the classes of 1939 to 1944. This long-term study showed the impact of parental relationships on health—warm and affectionate relationships translated into better health out-comes, lower adult anxiety, greater life satisfaction, and higher incomes. However, if participants in the study had strained relationships with either or both parents, they often had signifi-cant health issues, twice as often, in fact, as those that described their relationship with their parents as close. Thus, in addition to making it harder to find peace and happiness, an emotional and energetic distance from your parents may also exacerbate physical health issues

Vaillant also said that his study showed that "Happiness is love. Full stop." It's interesting to note that it is in receiving your parents' love, not giving it, that you access the ability to be loved. This is how you experience gratitude for life, aligning with the principle of *parents give and children receive* from the family energy field.

Yet, as young children, like Sam at fourteen, you want your parents to be happy. You want to give to them. When you see that your parents are sad or hear their tragic stories, you want to help. To heal their suffering, you might take on the roles of fam-ily caregiver, healer, protector, and peacemaker. Even for many adult children, this sense of obligation to take care of one's par-ents emotionally does not go away.

It's not just a son who might try to step in and fill the space left by his father. A daughter might step in to take care of her mother or her father.

Say a mother who did not feel connected with her parents tries to have her emotional needs met through her children. She might choose a favorite to make sure they don't abandon her and are loyal to her alone. She might be intrusive in asking for details about her children's lives and then not keep their confidences, sharing them with other siblings so they can feel "in the know" and "connected." Or maybe her youngest daughter takes on the burden of meeting her mother's emotional needs, in fact doing so willingly and feeling extremely protective of her mother's emotional safety and security.

But, when you go too far in trying to take care of your parents, instead of being able to receive your parents' love, you start to become an "over-giver." You lose your energetic boundaries and cannot practice self-care. Your locus or center shifts outside of you.

## Your Unconscious Blocks to Receiving

On the face of it, it appears honorable and noble to care so much for your parents—but it violates the flow of love from parents to children. If, like the daughter in the example above, you have to take care of your mother's feelings, at an energetic level, you start to disconnect from her and from yourself. Your referral point is no longer within you but outside yourself, and you evaluate yourself by other people's reactions. For instance, you might learn to anticipate and read your mother's expression and how she might react. (As my client said, "Being around my mother is like walking on eggshells.") You may no longer feel safe and secure. In your energetic field, there may be no room for your own feelings, just your parent's. You stop expecting your parents to be there to nurture you and respond to your needs. You stop expecting to be "seen."

You might extend this wariness from your parental relationships into your other relationships. Then, similar to the results of the study that George Vaillant found, you may not be able to receive love.

Sam was unable to receive the comfort, reassurance, and love he needed as his mother grieved. In a role reversal, he started to take care of her. Now, as an adult, despite a deep need to be seen and loved, he could not receive love and comfort in a relationship. In fact, his girlfriend complained that he often kept her emotionally at bay. Based on the principles of the family energy field, we can see that he could not trust that she would be there for him.

When you take care of your parents emotionally, you are likely to overextend yourself. You might grow resentful and bitter. You may not trust that you can be visible, authentic, and nourished by your relationships later in life. Giving too much comes from feeling unlovable and unworthy of love. You may become an over-giver to avoid being rejected. You might over-give to your parents or even to someone else: your spouse, your kids, your employers, your boss, or your friends. To balance not taking care of your own emotional needs, you might rely on others to take care of you emotionally. Your parents take from you, and you may look to others to balance that through misplaced expectations.

In the presence of being unable to connect deeply with others and create loving relationships, you might do some of the following:

- Be unable to protect your boundaries and allow people to take advantage of you by taking your time, resources, credit for your ideas or work.
- Try to please people as you search for connection, ignoring your own needs.
- Place a great deal of weight on achievement, status, and power instead of intimacy.

- Have trouble letting people getting close to you, for fear of rejection and betrayal.
- Regard other people with suspicion and see them as dishonest and untrustworthy.
- Expect too much from others.

One day I was in a bad mood, and I noticed my daughter trying hard to take care of me and make me happy. As I snapped out of it, I tried to explain to her that it was not her place to make me happy. My daughter looked at me and said, "What kind of child would I be, if I didn't want to make my parents happy?"

We all want our parents to be happy *with us*. You love them, and having them be happy with you makes you feel loved and accepted. As children, if your parents are not happy, you feel that they are not happy with you. Somehow, you must be to blame—or at the very least, you must fix the problem. Their unhappiness becomes personal, and it feels impossible to separate yourself energetically from their grief. To feel loved yourself, you may take it on yourself to heal their grief or anger or sadness. But children cannot do this for their parents. No matter how old you are, you cannot make things "right." More simplistically, you cannot make them "happy." You cannot heal the trauma of the lineage that made them what they are. As the family constellations founder Hellinger said, the child who imagines he can heal the grief of his parents is "to put it bluntly, presumptuous."

Taking care of a parent emotionally, whether it's a mother or father, makes it difficult for a child to develop a healthy emotional interdependence with others—to *receive* as well as give love and nurturance. Later in life, it becomes a struggle for the adult child to live their own life. Emotional caretaking for a parent violates one of the primary laws of the family system. While you may want your parents to be happy, you have to realize that you cannot *make* them happy. While this might sound selfish, when you honor them, see their stories with compassion, you learn the lessons you came here to learn.

During our sessions, my client Lara began to realize that she gave a lot both in her professional and personal relationships. Extremely creative, she didn't receive the credit that was due to her in her professional work. Sometimes her ideas and contributions were usurped by her coworkers, and in frustration, she often quit or switched jobs as resentment would build. She felt invisible in the circles in which she belonged, her voice unheard, receiving very little positive feedback and encouragement, yet her quiet contributions and her presence were invaluable. Her relationships would commonly end in misunderstanding and bitterness. Finally, in a new romantic relationship, Lara came to me because she wanted it to be successful.

This time, though, she decided that she would also simultaneously work on improving her relationship with her mother. Even though on the surface, she had a close relationship with her, Lara wanted to feel her mother's love for her more deeply. When Lara was just a year old, her mother had left her with her grandparents because she needed to be at the hospital with Lara's little brother, who was born prematurely.

Although it was a temporary separation, and despite having been cared for by grandparents who loved her deeply, Lara developed an unshakable certainty that she was not important, and people could not be trusted. Much evidence had accumulated to support this idea, in her personal relationships as well as with her mother, who was critical of her and violated her trust by divulging her secrets with her siblings. And, in keeping with this belief, her last relationship ended because her spouse had cheated on her. There was enough evidence for Lara to believe that people would always leave her, always disappoint. This same mistrust was now being echoed in her relationship with her new boyfriend.

This time, however, Lara decided to shift her relationship with her mother, forgive her mother's behavior, and let go of the pain of the past. In addition to taking some flower essences, she decided to follow a very simple suggestion I offered.

I asked her to create a way to appreciate and celebrate her mother. She found a beautiful old portrait of her mother, some of her mother's favorite things, and a saying her mother loved. Lara faithfully visited this space daily, reflecting on her mother's life. She began to appreciate her mother and recognize that her mother had, for the most part, done the best she could. That was enough. Because she was in a process of forgiving (or accepting) her mother, Lara started releasing the negative, harsh, and judgmental story that her mother was immature and self-centered and replace it with gratitude for her mother's youthful zest for life that Lara found inspiring. Lara noticed that she had started creative dance at a later stage in life just like her mother had and how much she relished the joy of movement. She was able to see that her own love for art, dance, and creative expression were her mother's gifts to her and came to appreciate her inheritance.

As you let your defenses down, you may begin to taste the sweetness of life. Its juice drips down your chin onto your hands and runs down to your elbows. You are a child again—the child of your parents!

Lara's intentional work to give up the story of how her mother had hurt her brought a new gift. Before she had expected to be left all alone; she was certain that she was anything but important in the eyes of her mother and boyfriend. She was positive that neither would nurture her and saw everything they did through this distorted lens. And she always "proved" herself right. Previously, she was always checking up on her boyfriend, worried that he was cheating on her. Now this change in her relationship with her mother allowed her to more easily trust her boyfriend. For Lara, not only did trust blossom but also a profound appreciation and respect for both her mother and her boyfriend's gifts as well as their struggles.

All of this happened even though neither Lara's mother nor her boyfriend had changed. The person who had changed was Lara herself—she chose to see them differently, to give them a chance to not hurt her again, extending trust even though it felt risky to do so. She also began to appreciate her own creative talents and strengths. Looking back at her life, she began to appreciate her resilience, courage, and determination. She also noticed that she had the strength to pick herself up, and her experiences had given her the wisdom to trust herself to navigate her way in life. She began to find her self-worth.

You may be like Lara, who on the surface might have a close relationship with her mother, yet distance yourself from your parents out of fear that if you keep your heart open, they will hurt you. Withholding verbal and physical affection might make you feel safer emotionally, perhaps, but you may never receive the love you crave.

I hear echoes of this desire when I listen to my clients:

"It's always about her."
"She's so critical."
"No matter what I do, she's never happy."
"My father never thought I'd amount to anything."
"I was never good enough."
"She's so narcissistic."

I hear deep pain, vulnerability, and the profound desire for something more: for love without conditions, or not having to work to earn the love you desire. Ultimately, it is the wish to be loved just as you are. The words of my friend's young daughter ring in my ears: "When you criticize me, I don't stop loving you. I stop loving myself." Children of physical or emotional abuse tend not to trust others and assume that those they care about will eventually try to hurt them. Children who are extremely self-critical may also have parents who are quite controlling and self-critical themselves. Studies, such as those discussed in *Frontiers in Psychology*'s article, "Attachment Styles and Suicide-Related Behaviors in Adolescence: The Mediating Role of Self-Criticism and Dependency" (March 10, 2017), show that extreme self critics are much more likely to attempt suicide than others.

It is important not to underestimate the role parents provide just by loving their children. Since the potential for loving and experiencing happiness depends so much on parents, when in that role yourself, you don't want to cause your own children to reject you and themselves and endanger their own self-worth. You don't have to love perfectly; you just have to love responsively. Perhaps even now, you may not fully appreciate the expectation that children have of their parents for love and assurance. Painful childhood experiences can cause wounds that may need to be healed down the road, when they are able to look back at them with adult eyes.

Whether or not you are a parent, if you have lost your self-worth and rejected your parents, it is important that you understand how that happened so you can begin healing the original wound. You may never be fully healed, but just as "good enough" parenting can prevent you from having a gaping hole in your heart, progress toward healing might be enough to free you from old patterns of unhappiness and disappointment in your relationships, patterns based on feeling unloved and unworthy. You can also help shift these feelings within you through the flower essences listed at the end of this chapter.

## Honoring Our Parents

In most religious traditions, you are asked to respect your parents. The first of the Ten Commandments, for example, is to honor your parents. The Talmud commands that parents are to be treated with extreme reverence. In Islam and Hinduism as well, children have a moral responsibility to respect their parents. In Korean and Chinese families, respecting elders is considered to be the highest virtue, drawing from the Confucian tradition. In the Analects of Confucius, he wrote, "Filial piety (respect for one's parents) and brotherly respect are the root of humanity."

However, the concept of honoring or respecting your parents, or elders, is slowly dying as cultural values shift across the globe. In the past, even if someone's relationship with their parents was strained, there was social pressure to speak well of them and to show them respect in public. I think it's interesting that most religious texts ask you to honor your parents, although not necessarily asking you to love them. In some ways, this implicitly acknowledges the level of dysfunction that might exist in families that make *loving* your parents challenging.

In Tibetan Buddhism, Indian philosophy, and even traditional Chinese medicine, the heart is the residence of the spirit, the gateway to a higher consciousness. In all these traditions, the heart holds the energy of unconditional love and compassion for yourself and others. Yet, negative emotions can also constrict the energy of the heart chakra. As the record keeper of your life, your heart remembers the joy, pleasure, and moments of happiness you experience. It also records the sorrows, hurts, and grievances you experience. Jerry Kantor, acupuncturist, homeopath, and author of *Interpreting Chronic Illness*, even points to cardiovascular diseases and mental disorders, including bipolar disorders and schizophrenia, originating as pathologies of the heart.

Even if you don't remember an experience of being hurt or betrayed, your body—your heart—does. You instinctively armor up against the risk of being cracked open again. I believe this is because our capacity to receive love is fundamentally linked to our self-worth, to seeing ourselves as being lovable. Self-worth allows you to be vulnerable, to be open, and to let your defenses down. You trust that you can handle challenges and pick yourself up after setbacks. It allows you to lift the barricades that blockade your heart.

At the "heart" of most healing, I've found, is the need to heal grief or heartbreak. You can honor your parents by taking care of them physically, financially, and even energetically, recognizing that you cannot heal them emotionally. Understanding this distinction allows you to discharge the debt of life while still taking care of your own emotional health.

Your relationship with your parents affects your capacity to love others and be loved in return because your biological parents, *even if you have never met them*, are within you. Their lifeblood is in the hands that you reach out to touch your face and touch others, in the eyes through which you see the world with hope and disappointment, in the beating, optimistic heart that incessantly circulates this lifeblood, and in the determined or leaden feet with which you walk the earth. Their energy, their experiences, were within the two cells from which you originated. By honoring your parents for what they gave you and accepting what they did not or could not do for you, you can start the journey to healing.

## The Energy of a Mother's Love

My mother always wore bangles—a symbol of marriage—given to her by my father. My sister and I also wore bangles, but in our case, it was for fashion. We wore them and took them off when we wanted. One day, my mother was trying to buy my sister a gift for her milestone birthday. Every time I talked to her on the phone, she sounded tired and discouraged. Despite my resistance, she felt that she needed to give me something as well, especially since she would be traveling all the way to America for the momentousness of the occasion. Finally, my mother chose two bangles and gave them to me on her visit.

The white and yellow gold intermingled and fit each other so that they seemed like a thick bracelet rather than two bangles. Yet, a simple movement made them come apart. When I touched them, I thought of my mother and her deep desire to give me something that was not ephemeral—that would stay with me.

"I hope you'll wear these," my mother said. I knew she had thought about it a lot and searched hard to find a gift that I would value, driving through the hot and dusty streets to find something that I would like, just like she had for my sister's gift.

"I don't know if I'll wear them all the time, but I will wear them." My mother sighed. I knew what she was thinking: life was too short, and she didn't know if I would wear them. However, when I met Kristen, I was wearing them.

I walked into Kristen's office from the waiting room and drew my breath in sharply. The energy was palpable. There was a

Buddha in the corner with water flowing next to it from a table-top fountain. Matchstick blinds shuttered the windows, making it a little dark. There was a massage table and Kristen herself looked like she had stepped down from the realm of goddesses. Her radiant, kind face drew me in instantly.

"Nobody comes to my office unless they are in the midst of a big change," she said. Skeptical, I told her I wasn't planning to do a reiki session, but I had come to inquire about renting office space. Before I knew it, I was back in her office for a healing session. I had sprained my foot, and I hoped that other than pain-killers, reiki might speed up the healing process. Kristen ran her hand over my navel and my arm. Not touching, but sensing the energy radiating from me, her hand a few inches above mine. The sleeves of my sweater were pulled to my wrists. You could barely see my bangles.

"This bracelet has a grounding, powerful energy. It's like Amma's energy," she said. Amma is an Indian spiritual teacher and is often referred to as the "hugging saint" from the south of India. Kristen had a small picture of her in one corner. "Where did you get these from?" At first, I didn't know what Kristen was referring to. Then, I suddenly noticed my bangles.

"Oh," I said, "these were given to me by my mother."

"It carries a very powerful energy."

In that instance, I felt as if I could suddenly see. In the most silent, quiet, and powerful way, this energy from my bangles was a demonstration of my mother's love. I saw a grounding protection that came from her love—supporting me through my life. My mother had loved without hesitation and without holding back. After my father's death, she had worked hard to pick up the pieces of her life so that she would not be a burden to us. She had learned how to manage her finances to the best of her ability, taken art classes, joined a nonprofit, made new friends, and actively tried to take care of her health—none of which was easy in a society where this was not the norm for a widow. She was constantly challenging herself to come out of her comfort zone. Instead of leaning on us, she had deepened her faith to fill that empty space my father left behind. I could feel her deep love for my sister and me and let it wash over me, filling me. On Kristen's table that day, I felt I had been given a glimpse of the depth of my mother's love for me.

I remembered a story from Indian mythology. A young princess marries a blind king and in loyalty to him, she wears a blindfold from that point on. Later, as her warrior son goes into the biggest battle of his life, his mother asks him to come and receive her blessing after bathing in the river—just as he is. He walks from the river, wrapping his silk garments around his waist. She opens the blindfold to bless him, releasing all the accumulated energy from her years of sacrifice to protect him with her gaze. The only part that he protects from her gaze is where he remains vulnerable—around his hips and groin. Ultimately, he is injured on his thighs and finally killed in battle. This mythological story reminds me of George Vaillant's research—that the ability to receive parental love has health benefits. This is another reason why, if you are frustrated because you feel that your parents should understand you completely, you may try to be less critical and not take for granted what they do for you— you may not be able to see all they give you.

My mother wasn't given to huge demonstrations of affection like ending calls with "Love you!" the way I used the phrase to casually end conversations. Hers was a quiet, enduring love that had grounded me, guided me, and protected me, enabling me to journey far from home, start my own family, and love my children. When I wrap my arms around my daughter, the bangles encircling my wrist remind me what it is like to love and be loved.

Anngwn St. Just, Ph.D., a family constellation facilitator and social traumatologist, observes on her blog *Trauma and the Human Condition*, from her clinical experience that "those who have a strong positive connection to both parents, entire family of origin and cultural roots, have the most resiliency and ability to adapt and prevail under very trying conditions." If you have or had a good relationship with your parents and relatives, that's good news. If not, with the essences and working with your energy field, there is hope for overcoming these challenges. You are never powerless.

To experience joy, vibrant health, resilience, and fulfilling relationships, you need to try and repair your broken relationships with your parents within you. As Mark Wolynn puts it in his book, *It Didn't Start with You: How Inherited Family Trauma Shapes Who We Are and How to End the Cycle*, "It doesn't matter whether they are dead, alive, or in jail," because it is an internal, not external, connection that you are making and repairing. If they are alive, you can't get attached to seeing them change just because your feelings are shifting. However, when you decide to say, "This happened, but it doesn't define me," then you can start the healing process taking care of yourself and ultimately honoring yourself. As you release expectations and "accept" your parents internally, you release victimhood and return to your own center. You may also find that you release the resentment that can keep you stuck in old family patterns. You become less reactive and find your inner worth. This will affect all your relationships, not just your parental relationships. Importantly, if you have experienced personal trauma, I encourage you to find qualified external support for this journey.

By recognizing that you can heal the parental wounds within you, you can break the family patterns that hold you back from living the life you want. And ultimately, as Patricia Mercier, in her book *The Chakra Bible*, writes, "When the heart chakra is fully open to love, you want other beings to share in the love and peace of infinite awareness."

Rewriting your parental stories and shifting your response from victimhood to self-compassion, self-love, and self-worth can help you heal. Yet, this is a challenging exercise of the will and the intellect because it requires a softening in the heart—especially toward yourself. The essences listed at the end of this chapter will help you in shifting this pain you hold. You can turn to them again and again as you need more support.

## Journal Exercises

1. Write about the following questions: Do you take care of your parent—mother or father—emotionally? Do you try to please people, make others happy, or take care of others? Even at work?

2. How good are you at setting boundaries? Do you take care of your own emotional needs or do you expect others to take care of them for you?

## Visualization Exercise

This exercise builds on the visualization exercise in the previous chapter. If you feel ready for this, you can try it. Can you think of your father as a baby who was given life? Did he know love? Maybe, maybe not. Did he feel safe? Did he come to feel worthy of love and safety? Now visualize that little boy who was just a toddler so many years ago, receiving love and compassion, receiving the resources that he needed to thrive. Imagine doing the same for your mother. Imagine your mother or father receiving unconditional loving, parental energy and any other resources that they might have needed but were missing in their lives. Love, support, encouragement, kindness, loving advice, and guidance. Notice how they shift once these resources are available to them. If you're ready, now imagine that with these resources supporting them, your mother places her hand on your left shoulder and your father's hand is on your right shoulder. Behind them, imagine the loving universal mother and universal father energy that nurtures them and you. Take a step forward, visualizing that this divine energy guides them and you and your way forward.

## Altar Exercise

Can you create an altar to honor your mother or father (even if they are still alive)? Perhaps it could be a collection of images, a list of their sayings or words of advice to you, their favorite flowers, or some of their belongings that you have. Are there any gifts from your parents that have special meaning for you? Do you feel that they offer some kind of protection or "good luck"? If these items are small, you could also place them on your altar. You could light a candle before their photographs and perhaps reflect on what you might have received. Fill some water with Willow and Holly flower essences and place it on the altar. You might also take these flower essences during the time you decide to create this altar.

If you don't want to create one for your parents, you could make one for a grandparent or other relative, family friend, teacher, or anyone who supported you and who you feel impacts your family energy field.

## Release Your Parental Triggers

If you feel criticized, invalidated, hurt, bitter, or angry when you interact with your parent, pick one emotion that feels predominant, and choose the corresponding essence by looking at the Glossary at the end of the book or picking one from the list below. Use this flower essence for the next three weeks and observe how you feel. Each of these layers of emotion can start to shift. It's not the event or circumstances that cause you to feel the emotion, but your feelings about the event, person, or circumstance. In other words, it's not your parent "making" you feel invalidated or criticized, it is you unknowingly making yourself feel that way after having been triggered by your parent's behavior. You can change your habitual response by releasing your judgment, beliefs, or expectations. The flower essence that you choose will begin to shift the judgments and corresponding beliefs you hold. The same events or circumstances will no longer trigger the same reactions—or if they do, the feeling is likely to be less intense.

As you work with the essences, you may notice that you also experience similar feelings in your relationships with other people. For instance, if you feel criticized in your parental relationships, you are likely to feel criticized in relationships with other people, and perhaps even those who have some authority over you, such as the person you report to or work for. Keep note of these emotions as you journal your reactions in the next few weeks.

## Flower Essences

**Pink Yarrow**—helps you keep energetic boundaries and to be compassionate without merging with another person's emotions completely.

**Post-trauma Stabilizer**—a blend of beautiful soothing essences, although it does have a strong alcohol taste owing to the brandy used as a preservative. Dilute four sprays in water or a dosage bottle if you prefer.

**Sweet Chestnut**—lifts the burden when you feel you have reached the limits of your endurance and can't take it anymore.

**Mariposa Lily**—a mothering essence for healing the mother wound.

**Baby Blue Eyes**—an essence for healing the father wound.

**Star of Bethlehem**—for soothing the grief within. It is often also called a mothering essence. Tears, if they come, are opening your heart and will help you to let go of the grief.

**Oak**—good for people who serve others beyond the limits of their endurance, since this comes at great personal cost. Constantly serving others in this way leads to burn-out, especially if the motivation is a sense of duty. This essence helps you find your limits and open yourself to *receiving* help.

**Beech**—helps you tolerate the habits, shortcomings, mannerisms, and idiosyncrasies of your parents instead of being triggered by them.

*See Glossary for details about the essences; also on how to create Boundaries Formula and Self-Love and Self-Worth Formula.*

— NINE —

# Everyone Belongs
# in a Family

One of the most well-known studies on transgenerational stress was done on mice. In 2013, researchers at Yerkes National Primate Research Center, Emory University, took young male mice and exposed them to the smell of cherry blossoms while also giving them an electric shock at the same time. This created a conditioned response in the mice: fear of that particular scent. Their offspring, both second and third generations, exhibited this same response despite never having been exposed themselves to the smell before. This was true even when the next generations had no contact with the original mice that had experienced the trauma.

Although there are several animal studies of transgenerational trauma being passed down, there are no similar human studies concerning the transmission of stress to offspring, i.e., how stress affects the expression of the genes or other biological processes that are inherited. Yet, environmental stressors like famine, obesity, smoking, alcohol, and exposure to stress have been observed to have behavioral and biological effects on the offspring of a person who has experienced these things.

For instance, in an article titled "Intergenerational Transmission of Trauma Effects: Putative Role of Epigenetic Mechanisms" in *World Psychiatry* (Oct. 17, 2018), Rachel Yehuda and Amy Lehrner describe how the children and grandchildren of men who were exposed to famine had higher rates of obesity and mortality than the successive generations from men who hadn't had these exposures. Like the mice who were afraid of the smell of the cherry blossom in subsequent generations, we too pick up the unresolved energies of our ancestors and these are reflected in the emotions we feel—their frustrations, their sadness, their anger. We face the same blocks and challenges they did. We even pick up on their health and financial problems. Through these emotions and the repetition of patterns, we remain connected— even through death. Because of their attachment to us and the material earth plane, our ancestors become the primary blocks behind our failure to manifest our dreams and desires.

My client Paul's son was having recurring nightmares in which a woman is wearing a scarf that gets caught in a machine and begins to choke her. In the dream, Paul's son tries to free her but is unsuccessful and, ultimately, he's thrown in prison for murdering her by strangulation.

Paul believed there could be a connection between his son's recurring nightmare and a story from his family's past about a great-uncle who was hung for a crime he didn't commit.

"But what's really disturbing," he confided, "is that there's no way my son knows about my great-uncle because he died before my son was born. It's been a painful family secret no one talks about, and yet my son can't bear to wear a turtleneck, tie, scarf, or any other item that presses against his throat."

We discussed how the dream made sense from the perspective of family patterns and karma. Mark Wolynn, in his book,

*It Didn't Start with You,* described this phenomenon as when a person becomes "identified" with ancestors who have been expunged from the family's awareness. We tap into the secrets that run underground in our family, even if we never know about them consciously. We take them on energetically, behaving and feeling as if we were the wounded one or the one who did the wounding. Paul's son may have been experiencing the energy of the transgenerational wound in his waking life, feeling the need to keep his neck free of any pressure, as if to avoid the sensation of the executioner's rope as when his great-uncle was being hung. At the same time, his son was dreaming of being responsible for someone's strangulation, identifying as the perpetrator.

When I suggested this explanation as a possibility to Paul, he was open to the idea. To heal this karmic wound in the ancestral energy field that was affecting his son, I encouraged Paul to talk with him about his great-uncle. I also suggested that he perform a ritual—on his own or with his son or other family members—to honor their uncle as well as forgive those who harmed him. If not, a member of his family might remain energetically connected to the unhealed emotions—Paul's son or perhaps someone else.

He honored his great-uncle by acknowledging his place in the family, the sacrifice of his life, and also by trying to forgive those who hung his great-uncle and their descendants. Paul offered prayers for these departed souls and lit candles for them. The dreams stopped and Paul's son started to be able to have clothing around his neck—including being able to pull up a zipper on a jacket or fleece all the way up.

When people used to speak of someone being "possessed" by the spirit of someone who had died, they may be referring to a similar phenomenon as Mark Wolynn's term *identified*—how we experience symptoms and behaviors of ancestors. We could also say our energy has become entangled with that of an ancestor, just as Paul's story showed. The memory of being hung was passed down to Paul's son in a similar way that mice can pass down the memory of cherry blossoms associated with a shock. Howsoever such transmissions of memory work, I believe these inheritances are real. By working with that possibility, we can heal family patterns that affect us and our relatives, helping ourselves as well as future generations.

## Why Does This Happen?

In constellation work, I learned that the family energy field was vast and guided by certain principles. One such principle is that *everyone belongs in a family*. On the face of it, belonging implies that we all have a right to be part of our family. But belonging is more complicated than that, and family is a wider concept than the immediate group we imagine. The living and the dead also belong, as do those our lineage has harmed or in turn have harmed our family.

What does it mean for everyone to "belong" in the family? Everybody has a rightful place in the family, and if someone is excluded, it harms the family system. Life often challenges us, calling us to step into our higher selves, but sometimes, we are unable to find within us the resources to rise to the challenge and we succumb to external pressures. We compromise family principles to fit in with society. One instance of exclusion could be when a young woman in a traditional society gets pregnant outside of marriage before she is legally and financially independent. One family might banish her forever, another might force her to deliver the baby in secret and give it up for adoption, never speaking of the child or the pregnancy again. Both of these instances violate the principle that everyone belongs in the family, reflecting the idea that a family is a unit designed to nurture, protect, and provide safety and love through *inclusion*.

A pregnancy out of wedlock might be out of synch with traditional cultural and societal norms in many countries. If that principle of belonging is violated, and a member is excluded, a child born into a family energy system in a descending generation can experience the emotions or the fate of the excluded family member, as we saw in the case of Paul's son. We somehow believe that keeping quiet will make the past disappear. Yet silence can cause these secrets to reappear in the symptoms we experience.

As you work with your family energy field, you might find yourself becoming increasingly aware of your family's norms and the ways in which they conflict with principles of love, inclusion, or honoring and respecting differences, and that can be difficult and painful. You may start to recognize the power of fear and other emotions that keep family patterns alive, generation after generation, and feel the weight of the challenge of letting go of them. You have, in fact, begun the task of repairing your family energy field.

At the same time, belonging means that we acknowledge that some people may be part of our family even if we believe they have done something wrong—and even if our contact with them is limited or nonexistent. This is the polarity of the family energy field that we have to navigate—identifying with the unresolved energies of members that cause the unconscious repetition of patterns and then consciously expanding and releasing them through understanding, forgiveness, and compassion. In this process, you accept that the energy and experiences of previous generations affect the current family members.

In working with the family energy field, you do not have to be in contact with your family members. However, you may still find this process can bring up difficult emotions. You can work energetically through altars and by releasing the emotions that run in your family energy field such as jealousy, desire for control, fear of intimacy, manipulation, or jockeying for power, position, or money over relationships. While these emotions exist in many family energy fields, they can appear as a recurrent event or in relationship patterns in certain families.

Working with the family energy field can be difficult because your field of vision starts to shift. When this happens, we have been given insight into our situation, which allows us the freedom to choose who we can be. This is the point of departure for an internal journey as we can see matters in a new light, which grants us the possibility of freedom from our story. It is this shift in perception that allows us to move from automatically reacting to triggers to responding mindfully. We see a situation for what it is, and we see people for who they are, as well as our own strengths and weaknesses. This sudden insight can cause deep anguish, especially if we see the truth about a situation that we have been ignoring or tolerating for a long time. An awareness of how people, ideas, or our family of origin shape us can lead to what has been called a "healing crisis." This is often part of the journey of letting go of all that no longer serves us so we can make space for our authentic self to emerge. Flower essences can support you in shifting and moving through the emotions that might come up in this process (see the end of this chapter for a list and the Glossary for details).

## Our Hidden Legacies

In addition to acts of kindness and loyalty, the family energy field holds the unresolved energy of untold secrets, painful wounds, or tragedies, including shameful transgressions. It's not just people who have harmed us or who we have forgotten that affect us. Our hidden legacies include those our families may have harmed.

My friend Ann had returned from the funeral of a relative, where she'd met an aunt by marriage. The aunt discussed the poverty and hardships this branch of the family faced; she believed they were the result of a family curse. As a child, Ann had noticed that her father kept a small medal in a little box. When she asked about it, her father told her that they used to have a worker who lived with their family. He helped on the farm and with odd jobs around the house. When World War I began, he went off to fight in the war and received this medal for bravery. When the man came back from the war, he continued to work for Ann's family; he had no other place to go.

At the funeral, Ann heard the rest of the story: As the family fell on hard times and Ann's grandfather died, it was hard for Ann's grandmother to keep the small family farm going. Her older children left home to work elsewhere and sent her small sums of money to live, but it wasn't enough. By now the worker had grown old, so she decided to find a way not to support him anymore. She had someone send a "fake" letter to him from a town hundreds of miles away. The letter writer claimed that the old man had family that had discovered his existence and invited him to come and live with them. In great anticipation, he left to find his family only to find out he had been tricked. Bitter and hurt, the man never forgave Ann's family. He even cursed them before he died, brokenhearted at their betrayal.

I asked Ann to find the medal and create an altar, asking the now-deceased man to forgive her family for the suffering they had caused him. Placing the medal on the altar, she lit a candle and prayed for his soul to be at peace. She expressed gratitude for all that he had done for her family and prayed for his forgiveness.

Two days later, Ann got a phone call. A close friend was redecorating her family room and had come across a much-cherished ring Ann had lost. It had been missing for a long time. For Ann, this reappearance of a long-lost treasure was an acknowledgment: there was a shift in the unseen world. Mementos, phone calls, or photographs often seem like coincidences, but having seen this so often, it is almost like a signal from the family energy field of a healing shift.

The land of the living and the land of the dead are not separate. Perpetrators of crimes and victims—alive or dead—departed ancestors, children who died young—all affect the family energy field in the present. The dead need to be acknowledged, respected, and mourned. When they are at peace, then the living too experience peace. Taking action to heal the family system, even if you weren't the originator of the harm done to others, is an act of deep love and grace.

## The Elephants in the Room

The ancestral energy field may not always be ready to give up its secrets. Some incidents might be too painful to talk about, or we might want to protect our children from this pain.

It is my experience that secrets reveal themselves when they are ready to be healed, and even through dreams or flashes of insight or intuition. We, as the recipients of those secrets, may be in shock when they are revealed, and we might feel that our lives have been turned upside down. When family secrets or other incidents come to light, use your altar to release the entanglement you or your family might be experiencing. Entanglement, as I said earlier, is experiencing emotions or a repetition of experiences that are not your own.

My client Lisa and her siblings unexpectedly discovered that their younger brother was actually their half-brother. Years before, their mother had had an affair and become pregnant. Lisa and her other siblings could not understand why their mother was so harsh with them but always defended this brother, taking his side. Lisa knew that her mother was adopted, although no one in the family talked about it. Even though, in a departure from the transgenerational pattern, Lisa's mother never gave the child up, her secret affected everyone in the family system, from the way the children perceived their mother to the way she parented them. With a fracturing of relationships among siblings and with her mother, Lisa had come to see me. In addition to giving her flower essences to release her anger at her mother about the way she had treated her in sharp contrast to how she treated her half-brother, I asked Lisa to honor her biological maternal grandparents with an altar ritual. Since she had no photographs and did not know their names, Lisa honored them by lighting candles and placing flowers in their memory on her altar. In doing so, she felt a profound shift and inner sense of peace—a feeling of belonging in a family system. Using both flower essences and altars to honor your ancestors and flower essences can shift the way your parental stories live within you.

Other people can also become members of our family system, such as adoptive children, stepparents, and stepgrandparents. If either parent had a former love or if the previous relationship ended in animosity, death, or any other kind of incompleteness, these people belong too. Why is this? Because this energy, or rather, unresolved and perhaps hidden emotions, affect others in the family energy field.

For instance, even if we adopt a child or are adopted, our biological parents are part of our family field. We cannot pretend that they never existed, even if it seems kinder to our adoptive parents, even if we resent having been "given up," or fear facing the possibility that we weren't loved by them. It is better to honor them by accepting that if they felt they could have kept or taken care of us, they would have. If you are the parent of an adopted child, perhaps you could express gratitude for the gift of the child. Notice the way the parents live in this child's eyes, their hair. Tell the child that their parents must have been beautiful to have created this unique being. The parents were young children once, who struggled just as this child struggles. Biological and adoptive parents are both part of the family energy field, even if the biological parents are unacknowledged. However, even if it's challenging to create space for members that we do not wish to include, acknowledging them energetically allows the field to return to peace.

## Making Space for Everyone

I believe the principle of including so many different people in our family energy field teaches us compassion and helps us expand our hearts. The eldest niece of my client Susan was an at-risk child who was adopted. With her curly hair, big expressive eyes, and infectious laugh, everyone fell in love with her when she arrived as a three-year-old. Just before this niece's wedding, Susan's mother, Alice, was hospitalized for a lump in her breast that a biopsy had shown was malignant. However, the treatment for breast cancer meant that Alice would miss the wedding. Determined to be there, Alice checked herself out of the hospital; the treatment would just have to wait. After all, this niece was the first grandchild in this big, connected family. Love is the glue that creates the feeling of "belongingness" in a family, and Susan believed that it was her mother's love for this child that was the turning point. That week, Susan and her siblings insisted on having the slides of the biopsy re-read by another specialist. It turned out that the tumor was actually benign; Alice never went back to the hospital. To this day, Susan and her siblings are eternally grateful to their adopted niece, because not only were they relieved that the tumor was benign, they also would have always believed they were genetically vulnerable themselves to breast cancer. In honor of this niece, their families support at-risk children in different ways. They feel it's the least they can do.

To be family or behave like family is a choice we make. Creating space for all our family members expands our connectedness with others. Honoring the idea that "everyone belongs" allows us to experience an expansion in our field of vision and deep gratitude for the incidents of life that perhaps we would miss.

When you shift your energy, you can also shift those who came before you. Unknowingly, you are repairing the fabric of your family energy field. When I first met my friend Gauri, she had been practicing Kundalini yoga for many years, with a fairly intense daily practice of yoga, meditation, and chanting sacred verses. One day, as she did her practice in the morning after she woke up, she felt someone breathing in the room. The breathing came from behind her, but each time she turned around, there was no one. After several days, she slowly became aware of a feeling of gratitude around her. She started to hear the words,

"Thank you! Thank you!" and became aware of the spirits of her ancestors surrounding her. They were thanking her for her practice and the shift in her energy. Her energy shift was enabling them to move to higher frequencies too. In Native American and Indian traditions, when we shift, we shift those that came before us, up to seven generations before as well as seven generations after. Gauri's story has stayed with me all these years, evidence of our power to shift our ancestral energy field.

## Journal Exercises

1.  Secrets in Your Family

    Are there secrets that run in your family that you may or may not be aware of? Is there a secret that you hold? How do you think it affects the way you interact with others, or the way things are in your family? Whose version of the secret do you hold? What do you believe to be true about the secret? What would happen if you looked at the secret from the perspective of someone else in your family? What is the price of the secret that you all bear? If there are secrets that are too hard to bear, find a stone that will hold the energy of the secret and place it in nature—perhaps under a tree, or at the feet of a garden statuary, or throw it in a river. Or you may wish to write the secret on a piece of paper and burn it.

2.  Bringing Secrets to Light

    Secrets take time to reveal themselves. One way to identify a secret that runs in your family—or even a different perspective on a story that your family holds—is to do a version of the exercise suggested by Julia Cameron in *The Artist's Way*. Journal every morning on your family stories, allowing yourself to write without judgment or censoring yourself. Some prompts might include:

- Write about your immediate relatives. Are there specific stories that sum up each one?
- Write about marriages or relationships in your extended family.
- Write about traditions, rituals, or behaviors common in your family. You can start with: "In my family, we . . ."

## 3. Specific Stories

Is there someone in your family whose actions have reverberated in the family for generations? Did they bring dishonor or shame to the family that still affects everyone? Can you rewrite the story that you all hold? Is it possible to see this story with compassion, looking for the backstory that led to it instead of shame? Compassion releases shame and fear of rejection if others find out. Are you afraid that your children might repeat it? Can you learn the lessons of the family energy field through this person?

## 4. Who Belongs in Your Energy Field

Can you think of people you might include in your family energy field? Here are some people to think about: someone who did something for your family that has never been fully recognized or appreciated, or someone in your own family who did something that has not been fully honored. If we are to be at peace, we need to honor the child who was left with relatives when the parents fled a war-torn country or was not believed when they told of being sexually abused—those we have harmed intentionally or unintentionally. Think of anyone you might have harmed or might be aware of that your family might have harmed. How about someone who has harmed your family?

## Prayer

When you practice *tarpanam*, think expansively of your family energy field. It includes people the family does not speak of, are forgotten, or your family might have harmed—intentionally or unintentionally—as well as those who might have harmed your lineage. You can also ask for help in forgiving those who have harmed your lineage.

To honor an ancestor, or to atone for harm done, or simply to express your gratitude, you might want to make an offering that feels in alignment with the healing—whether it is an in-kind or financial donation to an orphanage, a homeless or animal shelter, a food bank, or even volunteering your time and services where needed.

## Altars

Light a candle and ask for forgiveness for anyone harmed, on your ancestor's behalf or family's behalf, and do this more than once. If you wish, you can donate something to compensate for the injury your family might have caused.

If someone has harmed your family, sometimes forgiveness may feel beyond what you are ready to do, but it may be helpful to think of it as something you are simply acknowledging the need for. As the Native American saying goes, healing does not imply that the past never happened, it simply means that it no longer controls us.

Sometimes, when you are struggling with certain emotions or thoughts, you can write them on pieces of paper and place them on the altar, asking them to be released. You can also use stones or objects such as crystals to represent these emotions. If you hold them, centering and grounding yourself, you might find there is a message or insight for you. This insight is an expansion in your field of perception, an "Aha!" moment. In order to access this space of expansive energy, make sure your altar is grounded with higher sacred frequencies. Sometimes ancestral energy can shift in a day, sometimes longer. I once asked a client to do an honoring practice for forty days. Trust your own intuition; it will guide you. Ultimately, the wisdom of your lineage will also help you; you will *feel* the shift within you.

## Family Discussion

If you have children, nieces, nephews, etc., share stories of your ancestors and family members with them—the lessons, the wisdom, and the principles you have learned—so that they can guide the next generation. Teach them to find the heroes in their own lineage. As you rewrite your own ancestral stories through the lens of resilience, compassion, and love, you too will find the inspiration for your life as well. This allows everyone who belongs to the family to be included, acknowledged, or honored. And, as you release the past, you start to create the life and relationships you want with the support of your family energy field.

## Flower Essences

**Sweet Chestnut**—will help if you feel the burden of a secret you are holding.
**Holly**—creates expansiveness and compassion in your heart.

**Red Chestnut**—when you are consumed with anxiety and fear for your loved ones.

**Chestnut Bud**—for learning the lessons of the lineage.

**Wild Oat**—helps clarity and direction come from our inner realm, not the outer world. It is the essence to use when you are uncertain of your path forward.

**Crab Apple**—helps release feelings of self-hatred, shame, and feeling unclean from the deepest core within us.

**Pine**—helps when feelings of guilt are disproportionate to what has happened in the past, even if you were not the perpetrator of harm. With Pine, you can let these feelings go!

*See Glossary for details about these essences.*

# PART IV

# The Journey Home

— TEN —

# The Path Back
# to Yourself

So far, we have talked about lifting the burden of family patterns by recognizing their existence and then releasing them by honoring our ancestors through altars and prayers. By shifting your emotions with the help of flower essences, you have been learning how to hold those ancestral stories within you with compassion and shift the way their energy lives in you and manifests in your life. Releasing victimhood and finding gratitude for the gift of your life is not easy. An important part of that journey is restoring that connection to yourself. When you restore it, this allows you to recover your self worth and self love. You come back home to yourself.

In this part of the book, I will lay out the path for restoring your connection to yourself. You are the blossom of your family tree. Your life is about finding the capacity to blossom. When you build that connection back to yourself, when you come home to yourself, you can bloom fully. And paradoxically, as we saw with Gauri's story about how her meditation led to feeling the thankfulness of her ancestors in the last chapter, when you restore your connection to yourself, you shift your ancestral energy field as well. This is the expanding circle of life.

## Karma and Grace

While the law of karma is always in play, there is also grace. Grace makes its presence felt through synchronicity. No matter how challenging things may be, we've all had moments when things seem to miraculously come together in unexpected ways. It feels greater than luck or coincidence and for which you feel blessed and grateful. These unexpected events feel profoundly meaningful and are difficult to explain in logical terms. This is synchronicity. Synchronicity allows you to see that you live in a friendly Universe and that life isn't just happening *to* you, it is happening *for* you. When I was growing up in India and faced a setback, my mother would always say, "I'm sure it's for the best!" I hated when she said that. It never took the sting out of the moment, but I know now that she was urging me to trust in a greater destiny even when the signposts on my well-planned path disappeared. Synchronicity allows you to see how you are being taken care of.

Sometimes, it's easy to see how you are being guided. For instance, I might be planning to do something, and little signs appear that give me direction or reinforce what I'm thinking. There might be a song on the radio with lyrics that suddenly reach out to me, a written sign on a wall or on the back of a truck that feels like a message, or even an animal sighting or encounter that makes me pause. I'm left with a sense that something magical is happening. Today, I have a new and deeper appreciation of these signals.

Sometimes, guidance and affirmation come from the animal world. My first of many synchronistic experiences with hawks came when I was on my way to a workshop. I happened to glance up and saw a hawk on the tree above. I had never noticed hawks before and didn't think much of it until a discussion came up in the workshop about the symbolism of the hawk with regard to insight and vision. Hawks reappeared in my life frequently after that as I searched for insights and answers. I notice that deep insights in my life are always accompanied by the appearance of a hawk soon after or even right away, as if to reaffirm that I'm on the right path. During the work for this book, I went for a walk in my neighborhood and a hawk was sitting on the sidewalk with a squirrel it had just killed. It stared at me and showed no signs of flying away. I knew this was more than a coincidence; the symbol of the hawk in my life was telling me something. That encounter unsettled me, but it also reassured me that I really needed to trust myself and take a step forward.

Animal symbolism has probably always been part of Indian culture and held a central place in Native American traditions as well. Even if you have never considered the possibility of animal symbolism in your life, you might notice that certain creatures appear to be a universal expression of an idea—such as the dove, which is a symbol of peace, or a dog, which is a symbol of loyalty. In other traditions, they might be specific. For instance, crows and ravens are viewed as connected to the ancestral field and considered to be keepers of the sacred laws. In family constellation circles, sometimes a crow or group of crows would make their appearance at the end of a constellation at the moment of healing. While you could dismiss it as a coincidence, in that moment, it felt significant. Their appearance felt like a message of gratitude from the ancestral world. When a certain animal crosses your path, it stirs your awareness in a way that supports, strengthens, and even heals your spirit. This awareness has been called "animal medicine," or in my case what I was getting was "hawk medicine."

Even if synchronicity is one of the ways the Universe shows us grace, you may not recognize it at the time. There may be long lapses before you can tie all the unplanned events in your life together and see how they were strung like a strand of priceless pearls—like my impulsive decision to study homeopathy, which led to meeting Colette that I described in Chapter 3, and her presence when I went into the ER. All those events, taken together, were markers on the way to a new life path. However, I had to go to the emergency room three times before I was willing to change my attitude, try something new, and open myself to receiving help in the unanticipated form of Chinese herbal medicine. I guess I was kind of stubborn. Outer challenges push you to open your mind to possibility. They help you see that perhaps your life is not meant to follow your best-laid plans, but that a greater plan may have been laid for you instead. When you do see these coincidences in hindsight, you see a coherence as you connect the dots. The seeds of the future were planted in the setbacks of the past. My impulsive decision to study homeopathy had been laid several years earlier in response to my toddler getting multiple ear infections and colds. Contemplating the web of interconnectedness of events that led up to the moment of deep awareness made it feel miraculous. As I opened myself up to the Universe, there was no need to search for miracles outside—they were happening within my consciousness. I started to see deeper connections between simple, ordinary events and moments. The twists and turns—shaping me into who I had to become—were like a grand conspiracy to get me on the path I had to be on.

When you start to believe in synchronicity, it is a way of releasing resistance to the flow of life. You open yourself up to receiving guidance and direction, trusting in a larger plan for your life and putting your faith in something bigger than yourself. Colette offered me a life lesson that day in the ER when she asked if I wanted to approach my life a different way. Letting go of my resistance to change was the start of my journey into a different world, launched with her through a study group for a course that I never studied.

As I look back, meeting her led me to deeply understand the power of synchronicity and surrender. Together, they create a willingness to believe in possibility even if you can't see beyond your nose. It's trusting setbacks, delays, coincidences, and being open to change, believing that the Universe is supporting you, letting it take you where you are meant to go. It's when you start to imagine possibility—for your life. As Søren Kierkegaard, the Danish philosopher, said, "Life can only be understood backwards, but it must be lived forwards."

If I had to put a name to the phrase "Everything happens for the best," it would be this kind of surrender that concedes that a greater power knows my needs and my journey better than I do. The more I was aware of it, the more I could trust the Universe.

Seeing synchronicity has deepened my faith. I no longer need to know where the path will lead when the signposts are unreadable—although that does not always stop me from *wanting* to know. I have also become more comfortable with setbacks, knowing that if things don't go my way, there is a reason behind it—a better way or simply something I need to learn. I can trust myself, knowing that mistakes and challenges are part of my growth. This shift in my attitude has helped me tolerate uncertainty and trust that I will gain insights and direction from the Universe when I need it. As Deepak Chopra, author, speaker, and alternative medicine advocate, writes in *Synchrodestiny:*

*Harnessing the Infinite Power of Coincidence to Create Miracles*, as you encounter "more and more synchronicities," the process accelerates to a point where you actually experience it as miraculous. Family constellation therapy acknowledges synchronicity in the constellation process as well. Representatives who are chosen by the client share an element of the client's story in their lives; participation in the process allows them to heal a story or belief that they have been holding on to. Sometimes this connection is clear, while other times, it is not obvious till much later.

## Faith Takes You Beyond Synchronicity

Synchronicity is a building block of faith—teaching you to surrender more easily. But faith takes you beyond synchronicity and gives you hope because it may take years for you to really see the whole picture. In the long lapses before you can connect the dots together and make sense of the path of your life or start to see the outcomes and changes you want to see, faith sustains you.

Faith expands your field of awareness, bringing you into the present, releasing the anxiety of the future. Faith does not require the existence of religion, although religion is, of course, compatible with faith. When you say you must take a "leap of faith," it really does mean taking that leap beyond what may be observable or even known to you. It sustains you with hope and optimism when setbacks and failures occur, when there seems no end to your suffering. If the storms of life are inevitable, faith helps you weather them. As you build faith, you can open yourself to receiving your life, accepting its challenges, and despite them, feel that you are being taken care of—that you are being held in infinite tenderness by an invisible world.

I believe that hope is the magic stardust and gift of faith. Hope allows you to be patient with the gap between your expectations and reality, whether it is in your daily life or your long-term goals and aspirations. You may underestimate how long it takes to learn a skill or change your behavior, but you can know enough to be patient and persistent. Hope is fundamental to life and inextricably linked to faith. Hope, in fact, is the hardest love you carry for *yourself.*

In Indian astrology, the transit of the planet Saturn, or Sani, is considered a "malefic" that brings a series of bad events. For instance, you could lose your job, get divorced, and then end up in a car accident. Such a pile-up can leave you feeling helpless, and some of these may not be the result of your own actions. And yet, when the planet Saturn transits your astrological charts, you are in the deepest learning zone of life. Its influence lasts almost eight years. Long enough to mature and grow in strength—or become bitter. In astrological parlance, Saturn is considered the greatest teacher—the planet of karma and responsibility. As I said earlier, I never really understood how the planets and different "houses" in the charts influenced each other, and I was never drawn to learning astrology. However, I did learn that when you expect challenges to happen, rather than block your awareness of their possibility, you are developing the essential spiritual skills of optimism and patience. The prevalence of astrology in India meant that people carried an awareness that life would be challenging at times and might even be difficult for a long stretch. The prescriptions that astrologers offered often asked you to deepen your faith through recitation of certain prayers depending on the challenges you were facing. The long lines around the Sani or Hanuman temple are testimony to the challenges people go through and their faith-based response. Faith gives you hope.

Why did they go to the Sani or Hanuman temple? The story goes that Hanuman was utterly devoted to his master, the legendary archetypal Eastern hero Ram, who remains calm through adversity and challenge. Sani placed his foot on Hanuman, who did not flinch. No matter how much he pushed, he could not crush Hanuman's will or spirit. This is why many people visit the Hanuman temple in India, honoring the archetype energy of indomitable spirit against all odds. The spirit of hope, faith, and devotion helps you keep that connection to yourself and to life—even when challenges overwhelm you.

## The Challenge of Building Faith

I've heard it said that it's easy to be religious, but difficult to be spiritual. Religion, to me, is about believing in God, or a higher power, for lack of a better word. But spirituality is about experiencing that connection. It's not about changing others or getting others to believe in something, it's about changing yourself. While religious traditions might differ, the experiences on the mystical or spiritual path are very similar, irrespective of religion. In each step of that journey, you are building that connection to yourself—or what you might call your soul or higher self. When you are tired of religion, it's easy to jettison the baby—belief in a higher power—along with the bathwater. And when you do that, you also jettison that deeper connection to yourself.

However, when you are tired and want to make meaning of your world, you can also open yourself to searching for that connection to something bigger. The act of doing that connects you to yourself and to hope. Sometimes I experience a sequence of frustrations. I can't put my finger on it, but there appears to be a common underlying pattern to them. For instance, I might be allowing my boundaries to be violated in the same way by the same person each time. Or I might be triggered by someone's behavior that seems out of proportion to the situation. At that time, I might not be aware of what's going on and simply feel angry or frustrated. I can't name the emotions that are coming up that are underlying my anger and irritation, and I can't see what's going on. But if I start to reflect, I start to become aware that through these patterns and these emotions, the Universe is trying to bring something to my attention. That is the moment I become aware and need to go within. I need to understand the pieces of me that I am trying to weave back together into coherence. I keep asking myself the questions, "What do I need to see? What do I need to learn? What do I need to understand? What is my resistance to?" The answers to these questions may not show up right away, but the more open I am to receiving answers, the more I am able to receive guidance from the Universe. When I experienced this series of frustrations, I realized that I was not being forthright about the extra help I needed to manage the demands that were being placed on my time. Knowing that everything is part of my journey allows me to stay hopeful and optimistic, and the answers are the catalyst for a deeper connection with myself, allowing me to trust and accept life. From that space, it's easier to accept others.

When you're frustrated, sad, anxious, or irritable and have given up on organized religion, perhaps it's time to open up that connection to the invisible world and to yourself. You might feel that things are not going your way, your relationships are lacking, and what you want appears out of reach. While I didn't have to think about building my faith, it was challenging sometimes to keep my faith when times were tough. But, since it was the only thing I knew, I leaned in deeper on it. If you are starting out, there are many ways to build your faith. If you have created an altar, you can stop before it with gratitude. You can begin by noticing little blessings. If you have given up on prayer, perhaps you can simply start those conversations again. You could journal to a higher power or simply ask for those you love to be taken care of. You might even go back to your religion or religious texts with fresh eyes. If you are resistant to believing that there is something kinder and greater that takes care of you, you might lean into your resistance to learn why that happened and when it happened.

Challenges, frustrations, and setbacks are part of your growth in ultimately trusting that you can pick up the pieces of yourself and reclaiming the power you may have given away to others in the past. If you are looking to deepen your faith, synchronicity is a magical ingredient. As you notice synchronicity, you keep the flame of hope alive—for yourself, for your life on earth—and gratitude for this gift of life. As my teacher would say, you can see the magnificence of creation in a blade of grass. Faith, synchronicity, and hope are linked together.

If you start searching for synchronicity, you start living with expectations, but when you simply start *experiencing* synchronicity without searching for it, you are living in the flow. It's a way of shifting your awareness into an expansive state. Being aware of synchronicity increases your capacity to hold life's challenges. It's like seeing life simultaneously through a microscope *and* a telescope. It is not forcing events that you see to conform to or justify a point of view you are holding, but rather, when you experience synchronicity, it leaves you with a sense of magic and wonder, and you feel a re-enchantment of your daily life. Synchronicity, as I see it, is a partnership with the Universe and in so doing, you are cocreating destiny. With faith and hope, you begin the journey to reclaiming the power you may have unconsciously given away.

## Journal Exercises

1. If you look back at your life, what choices did you make based on the challenges that you were dealing with? These choices are turning points in your life. Did they take you down a path that was unexpected? Where are you today based on those choices? How did they shape you into who you are today? What did you learn from the choices you made? How did they shift your view or philosophy of life? You can also examine the choices you made based on the gifts you received in your life—whether they be family, wealth, opportunity, faith, skills, or talents. How do they play a role in your life? Do you take them for granted? Sometimes, it's hard for you to see what you have received because you have not seen life without it. You can't imagine how your life would have been without these gifts. Notice how these gifts have shaped you so that you can experience the little or large blessings in your life.

2. How hopeful are you? Do you see challenges as an opportunity to learn, or do you berate yourself for being a failure? Do challenges overwhelm you? Optimism is a learned skill when you begin to see the gifts of the challenges you are facing.

## Animal Symbolism Exercise

Animals that appear at unexpected moments can create that sense of wonder in your life. Are you drawn to certain animals? Do you collect figures of them—such as rabbits or elephants? Have you ever wondered why you might be drawn to a particular animal? You can research the symbolism of this animal, and I invite you to notice the way it makes appearances in your life. As you start to notice one or more animals, you create a connection to the natural world around you and build that sense that you are being held and taken care of.

## Synchronicity Exercise

In order to see synchronicity, you need to simply build awareness. Just notice what is going on in your day with a sense of detachment and without judging it. If something didn't go your way, don't think of it as good or bad, just accept it and notice what happens without expectation over the day, or over a longer time. When you are mindfully aware, you allow yourself to notice small connections, gifts, and blessings: it's how you start to notice how magical life is. You can also look at a person in your life, a skill or talent that you have, and reflect on how it came to be. How did this person arrive in your life? What coincidences played a part? How did you become good at something? What circumstances played a role?

## Flower Essences: An Optimism Formula

**Gorse**—for hope when things feel hopeless, and you feel helpless.

**Gentian**—for lifting you up in the face of setbacks and discouragement.

**Larch**—for giving you confidence to take risks and try new things.

**Sweet Chestnut**—for when you feel that there is no end to your suffering and that you are at the end of your rope; when you "can't take it anymore."

**Elm**—for feeling overwhelmed by the things you have to do.

**Wild Rose**—for apathy and loss of interest in life.

**Willow**—for bitterness if you feel like a victim.

**Impatiens**—for patience with the larger timetable of life.

*See Glossary for details about these essences.*

# — ELEVEN —

# Connecting with Mother Earth

The earth is your true Mother, providing you with water, food, air, and healing herbs and flowers. Even flower essences are nature's way of healing our emotions. Our remains, whether you are cremated or buried, never really leave the earth. Its energy matrix holds unfathomable, unspoken memories of the human race.

If being able to receive the love of your parents and others and trusting in the love and support of the Universe brings you back to yourself, being able to receive the loving energy of the earth also brings you home to yourself, your body, and to being on earth itself. While shifting your internal relationship with parents is very challenging, I encourage you to try and connect with the nurturing energy of the earth.

Our ancestors honored their connection to the earth. Simpler lifestyles connected people to the land, with its natural, nurturing, and gentle electrical energy. But, like your connection with your ancestors, your connection to the land can be lost. Consequently, you too can become, as Buddhist philosopher Thich Nhat Hanh said, "lost, isolated, and lonely."

According to the UN Refugee Agency, in 2020, there were nearly twenty-six million refugees in the world, almost half of them under the age of eighteen, and almost eighty million people had been forced to flee their homes. With these distressing numbers, you can only wonder who is at "home" on earth. Looking at it from another perspective, with alarming rates of obesity, people today also struggle to feel at "home" in their bodies. And if you feel that you were born into the wrong family, you can see why it may be hard to find a place to call home. For many of us, coming home to ourselves and feeling safe and at home on earth and in our bodies can be a long journey. As an immigrant, the sense of displacement I felt was deeply unsettling. But, just like connecting with your ancestors, by connecting with the energy of the earth, you can start to heal yourself and feel a sense of "home" wherever you are.

When I was growing up in India, my father would often send us outside in the morning.

"Go and walk on the grass barefoot! It's good for your eyes," he would say.

In the hot summer morning, the grass, wet with the morning dew, felt cool beneath our feet. When we went indoors, our feet would dry quickly on the marble veranda. When we weren't barefoot, I liked to wear my Kohlapuri flip flops—those handmade leather sandals from the village of Kohlapur—more than the ones made of rubber. In the summer, we practically lived in them. We didn't know it then, but by walking barefoot in the grass and by wearing leather sandals, we were connecting with the energy of the earth.

In India, it is inherently understood and accepted wisdom that you are nourished by the land—and even more so if you are on a spiritual path.

My connection to the earth didn't end when I left to live in the US. On a recent trip to Yosemite National Park, we had two young guides. They had come to work in the park as students, one from Rhode Island, the other from Iowa, but both had stayed even after they no longer were in school because their love for the land and the forest was so deep. They felt they'd come "home."

We smelled the bark of the trees—pine and cedarwood.

"Mom! The bark does smell like butterscotch!" my daughter called out to me.

I inhaled the distinct sweet fragrance. We touched the trees. It felt wonderful to be together as a family, in nature, and in harmony. My system calmed down. We sat by the stream and watched the water flow; we could have stayed there forever. Giant redwood trees towered above us; we were insignificant next to them. And they would still be there when we were gone, but in their presence, it felt sacred and wondrous to be alive.

Standing on a plateau in Yosemite, I suddenly remembered Teji's story. My friend Teji was an avid mountaineer, and a doctor by profession. With this winning combination, he was often in demand by mountaineers who needed a doctor for their high-altitude climbs.

Many years ago, on one of these expeditions in the Himalayas, Teji and the men with whom he was climbing tied themselves to one another to cross a glacier. Weighed down by their equipment and clothes in those freezing temperatures, they had to walk very slowly to avoid the deadly crevasses. In the distance, they could see something coming toward them.

It couldn't be an animal, not at this altitude. Thoughts of the yeti crossed Teji's mind.

What could be moving toward them?

As it came closer, they saw it was a man. Clad in a loincloth, bare-chested and barefoot, he walked across the glacier, smiled at them, raised his hand in blessing, and continued walking.

"At that moment," Teji told us later, "I felt the weight of everything I was carrying. My clothes, the pickax, and everything else."

I have always been fascinated by this story. I knew that yogis are reputed to have lived in the mountains and forests of India for thousands of years. This was the first time I had heard of anyone I knew meeting an actual yogi, living lightly, one with the land, nourished by it, untouched by the heat and cold.

I looked at the delicate silver river in the valley below, flowing between the peaks on either side. Sunlight sparkled on the water, and I felt a sense of amazement at how this shimmering silver ribbon nurtured and protected such a vast expanse of land, sustaining millions of people.

"Has anyone ever lived in the park?" I asked our naturalist guide.

"Yes, a man did live here. Sometimes he would ask the climbers for a little salt, so people knew about him."

"What happened to him?"

"The forest rangers found him and made him leave. I hear he is now a homeless man on the streets of San Francisco."

After we went home, I thought more about this. Maybe we can't legally be nomads on the land anymore, but the principle of living close to the earth and living lightly still applies. I often had my own kids play barefoot in the yard to teach them to ground and connect with the earth like I had been taught.

## What Does It Mean to Be Grounded?

In spiritual terms, the feeling of being connected to the earth, being present and balanced, is often referred to as being *grounded*. When you meet someone who is grounded, they seem thoughtful, practical, capable of handling a crisis and their everyday affairs. Massage therapists and people who work in the healing field often ground themselves to protect their energy from getting entangled with their clients'. In family constellation workshops, there was a lot of emphasis on keeping your energy field intact and preventing it from getting entangled with ancestral energy.

There are several ways to "ground" yourself, protect your own energy field, and become calmer by connecting with the earth's energy. You can sit outside in nature, walk on the grass barefoot, take Epsom or magnesium salt soaks, use "grounding" flower essences, do yoga, or use visualizations that help you connect with the energy of the earth. When you are grounded, the locus of your energy is centered within you despite the challenges around you.

One morning as I got ready to drop my daughter at school, she looked at me and said, "Mom, I don't think you are grounded." The look on her face was very serious.

"I know!" I felt very spacey. I had slept little for several nights, had been overworked for several weeks, and now it was Monday morning! I was having trouble keeping track of what I was supposed to be doing, and I couldn't seem to get her breakfast together. I went upstairs and I couldn't remember what I had come up for. I couldn't find my glasses. I left my keys somewhere and couldn't remember where.

"I don't want to get in the car with you till you're grounded," she said.

"I think I'm going to be fine," I said. "Let's go! You're going to be late." I was tired, stressed, and couldn't seem to focus.

That afternoon, I picked her up from school, entered the little road that segued into the ongoing traffic, and stopped at the yield sign. I watched to see if the traffic would let up. There was another car ahead of me that was also waiting. The traffic eased and I accelerated. Crash! I heard the grinding of bumper on bumper and felt my body jerk!

"Mom! You're not grounded! Did you ground yourself?" my daughter cried out.

"I guess not!" My hands flew over my ears and face in horror at what I had done. Although I felt better after the caffeine, it had been a busy day and I had not taken time to center or ground myself.

No one was injured, and the damage to the other car was not overwhelming. Yet, when I was not grounded—even my young daughter could tell! You start to recognize the symptoms. That incident was a stinging reminder to practice what I was teaching her.

We can become ungrounded because of stress, anxiety, or lack of sleep. In addition, being constantly on digital devices and electronics also causes us to disconnect from ourselves as well as from the energy of the earth. The gravitational force of the earth allows you to live on her surface, enabling your spirit to reside in a human body. When you are grounded, you also return toxic or waste emotions to the earth. When you are not grounded or rooted, you cannot expel them. Think back to when you may have taken a walk as you mulled over an issue that was bothering you and how you felt after you returned. When you sit outside in nature, watch the sunset or the sky, notice the birds that fly, touch the trees, or bring flowers into your home, you are consciously building a connection to the earth. When you actively do this, you open yourself to gratitude and receiving.

All over the world and throughout history, the earth has been commonly referred to as a feminine nurturing energy: Mother Earth versus Father Sky. As we become more scientifically advanced, we have moved away from the term *Mother Earth*, and with it, we break the link with reverence and awe.

Astronauts who have been to space often experience a shift in their awareness of the beauty and fragility of the earth, speaking of their astonishment that the earth is actually alive, just as alive as all of us are. They describe their wonder not just of discovering space, the moon, and other planets, but of seeing their own planet in a new way.

The astronaut Ron Garan said, "When you look down at the earth from space, we see this amazing, indescribably beautiful planet. It looks like a living, breathing organism. But it also, at the same time, looks extremely fragile . . . it's really sobering to . . . realize that this little paper-thin layer is all that protects every living thing on earth from death, basically. From the harshness of space."

We send people into space to discover the moon, nebulae, other galaxies, but what these brave adventurers are saying is simpler than that: you really discover the value of your home, the earth! These moving tributes by the astronauts remind us that Earth is delicate, warm, touchingly alone, small, and irreplaceable. They ask us to stop mistreating the earth, but rather love and cherish her.

By shifting our conscious loyalty to Mother Earth, we open ourselves to being nurtured.

# The Healing Power of Water

I remember going to India and watching the evening prayers or *aarti* by the Ganges River. People lit their little oil lamps and against the backdrop of bells, chants, and the darkening sky and water, they sang to the water. *Pushkars*, annual rituals of love and gratitude that honor your energetic connection to the earth, are performed along the banks of the twelve rivers in India in rotation, and villagers come forward to touch the swiftly flowing water and then touch their foreheads in reverence. Reverence for water is found in almost all native traditions. Throughout the world, there are sacred sources of water as diverse as the spring that comes from the grotto at Lourdes, Cenote Sagrado in Mexico, Lake Atitlan in Guatemala, Lake Mansarovar in Tibet, holy wells in the British Isles, and rivers and springs in the United States that were sacred to the Native Americans.

Masaru Emoto, Ph.D., in his book *The Hidden Messages in Water*, describes his groundbreaking theory that water has consciousness. He froze water after exposing it to the written or spoken word or music. Emoto then captured the changing crystalline structure of water using a powerful microscope and high-speed photography. His study of water showed that thoughts, feelings, and even music affect reality. Water that had been exposed to loving words showed startlingly beautiful, complex, and brilliant snowflake-like patterns. Water, on the other hand, that was exposed to harsh words, written or spoken, failed to crystallize. Polluted water also failed to crystallize with incomplete or asymmetrical forms and lacked brilliance.

His work showed me the power of words. Harsh words make their way across generations, becoming visible in constellations or in my client work and preventing us from reaching our potential by undermining us from within. But Emoto's work also gives us an inkling of the latent power within us—power that can be used for healing and peace—by choosing your thoughts and your intentions. Like Emoto's theory that water when prayed to changes its crystalline structure no matter how polluted it is, prayers of gratitude to our ancestors can shift our family energy fields. Like Mother Nature, gratitude is an expansive energy. When you look through the eyes of gratitude, you see opportunity in your challenges. Gratitude can also make it easier to honor your parents for what they were able to give you rather than what they couldn't.

For some in modern society, the breakdown of the extended family structure, unexpected hardships, financial losses, or divorce can leave children and surviving parents vulnerable. It might be challenging to access feelings of abundance, strength, and financial or physical security—emotions that lead to a reduction in stress and anxiety. In these situations, it can be difficult for a person to draw on the positive energy of what has been called a "prosperity consciousness."

To access feelings of security and sufficiency, you have to go within. This might sound like a contradiction, but these feelings have less to do with material possessions and more to do with an attitude of appreciation since they help you access the energy of abundance. When you feel grateful, you can even be generous with what you have—however little—and trust in the flow of life.

Several years ago, my family and I visited the temple of Kwan Yin, the Buddhist Goddess of Compassion in Penang, Malaysia. Kwan Yin holds prayer beads in one hand and in the other, a small jar that contains the nectar of compassion. After visiting the temple, we made our way down to the parking lot. Beggars lined the side of the walkway. Some were old, some infirm, but some were young. As we walked, my son gave some money to an old woman who was begging for spare change. Close on his heels was my daughter, and she gave her some too. The old lady shook her head and with a toothless smile, she motioned for my daughter to give the money to an old man my daughter had already passed. My daughter went back and put the money in the little tin bowl in front of the man. As the coins clinked and rattled against the metal, I realized that, in the most gracious way, the woman had taught both me and my daughter how "enough" is simply a state of mind.

When you feel you have enough, you can be generous and trust in the flow of life and abundance. This beggar woman could have pushed my daughter to give her more money. Instead, she nudged her to consider being generous by giving the money to the other man. The late therapist Boszormenyi-Nagy found that those who could show generosity toward others experienced an increase in self-worth, inner freedom, and physical well-being. As you live more lightly on Earth, you can slowly make the journey to feeling not just that you *are* enough, but you *have* enough.

## Walking Meditation Exercise

Go for a thirty-minute walking adventure in your neighborhood as if it was a pilgrimage. Trust your instincts and your intuition to guide you on this journey. Walk slower than usual. Notice which way you are being guided to walk. To turn left, or right? Notice the color of the sky, the nature of the clouds, the shape of the trees, the width of their trunks, the texture and subtle shades of bark, the way they might peel and create patterns. Do you want to reach out and touch them? Notice the dappled sunlight that makes some of the leaves brighter than others, creating different shades of green. Notice if the trees have berries or seed pods, and how leaves are all so different from each other, and the graceful lines of the branches. Notice the flowers, if there are any, even those humble, determined, fierce ones that grow through the cracks on the sidewalk. Notice the shadows on the ground—dark and light—animals that scurry around, the birds that fly, and their sounds that accompany all this activity. Notice the people that you might see and if you choose to acknowledge them. Sometimes even boarded wooden windows, whitewashed walls, and cement blocks can have subtle detail and texture as beautiful as any abstract painting. Be open, curious, and adventurous. Drink in all the details that you can. Let go of judgment and see if you can appreciate all that you see around you—the nature that surrounds you, and anything you might encounter.

When you return, write down your impressions in your journal, including how you feel.

## Connecting to Water Exercise

Water as a symbol is often used to represent the watery depths of your emotions and is also connected with the principle of flow. Rock Water is a "flower" essence (not derived from flowers but part of Bach's collection of flower essences—see Chapter 5 for more information or the Glossary at the end of the book) that releases rigidity in your thoughts and ideas, such as when you have standards so high that they paralyze you, leading to procrastination from fear of failure. While you can take the essence orally, you can also fill a tub with water and put twenty drops of Rock Water essence into it. Energize the water by moving your hand in a figure-eight infinity loop pattern, which represents rhythm or flow. Step in and let the water soothe you!

You can also tape positive words to your drinking water bottles—*gratitude, harmony, balance*—or symbols such as for the archangels. If you use a deep-blue bottle, you can solarize the water by placing it in sunlight for half an hour. Notice if you feel any changes when you drink this water. I have several such bottles, and I notice that this water always hydrates me more than any other water I drink.

## Flower Essences

**Hornbeam**—for procrastination when your energy seems "stuck." The act of emptying closets and getting rid of stuff is often your way of signaling to the Universe that you are making space for something new. It suggests that you are ready to invite change. I'm always surprised at what I might tackle on my to-do list with a little bit of Hornbeam! Sometimes, you might discover as I did, it was not on my list, but on my mind!

**Honeysuckle**—for helping you let go of the past and of hoarding. Couple it with Hornbeam to let go of procrastination, possessions, and the past.

**Grounding Green**—for building your connection to the earth, helping you become deeply aware of it and be nourished by it.

*See Glossary for details about these essences.*

# — TWELVE —

# Let Your Life Blossom

What simple action can you take for yourself that also lifts the burden of any family legacy you carry? Just as a one-degree shift in direction can chart a whole new direction for a gigantic cruise ship—similarly, one small persistent change can potentially create dramatic changes in your life and in the family dynamic you carry. That action, I have come to realize, is taking responsibility for and honoring your life.

Rather than taking it personally when you realize you've been born into a family that has suffered for generations, you can seize your opportunity to bring about healing regardless of who or what inflicted the first trauma that set your family patterns in motion. You may, in fact, never know what set the pattern in motion. The ensuing trauma will be held in your thoughts and cellular memories, passing down from generation to generation, if you don't face the issues of the past.

Moving beyond the limitations imposed on your life by the family energy field requires you to not just honor your ancestors, but importantly, also to take responsibility for your life and honor yourself.

# What Does It Mean to Honor Your Life or Yourself?

Taking responsibility for yourself is to release victimhood and the stories that imprison you in the past and prevent you from creating the life you want. When you honor yourself, you can take care of your feelings, noticing the messages they have for you and recognizing the power you have to heal the parental wounds you carry. It means that you have compassion for your journey and recognize the gifts of growth in the challenges you have been through. It's recognizing that the journey of life is to move beyond the stories that have limited you. And, in doing so, you can even be compassionate toward others.

As you choose to take responsibility for your life, no matter what your life circumstances, with persistence, faith, optimism, and courage, you can reclaim your self-worth. When you speak from this place, your words emerge with nonviolence, kindness, and respect; your voice is no longer a battleground between the emotions you want to experience and those you end up expressing. As Gauri's commitment to her yoga/meditation practice showed in Chapter 9, you even heal your roots when you commit to yourself; you shift the burden of the lineage you carry.

# Shifting Your Perspective

Trapped energy—which is your long-standing unsupportive beliefs, repetitive thoughts, and overwhelming emotions—can keep circling endlessly within you like a goat tethered to a pole. Below the waves of emotions, you can start to see the seabed of beliefs that are holding you locked in this situation. Questions are your gateway out, and within them are the seeds of the answers you seek. When you are persistent in your search, intelligence and grace can enter the system from outside, and this will begin to interrupt the energy from circling repetitively. The system will expand to hold these open questions, and the solutions or answers you *demand* will allow you to move beyond your limiting situation.

For instance, when I left Chicago and moved to Boston, I was offered a position at a university, similar to what I had been doing before. However, by then I was moving away from the world of academia. The offer was tempting, and I pondered over whether I wanted to take the job.

"Do you want to tie yourself to an anchor or a rocket?" my friend Robin asked.

"A rocket!" was my quick reply.

"So, is this opportunity an anchor or a rocket?"

"It feels like an anchor," I said. I felt weighed down and boxed in by the idea of doing the same work I had been doing. I became aware that the disconnect between the heart and the mind in my work was keeping me unfulfilled. The question Robin asked helped me make my decision.

Questions open you to the act of observing deeply. Your willingness to look at the situation while suspending judgment is expressed through them. When you observe something—a person, a situation, or even an event—in a different way, you can see it from a new angle, perhaps even multiple angles.

Having made that decision, I entered that liminal space where I was stripped of a job title, but I didn't yet belong to myself. I was no longer in that well-defined container where I could tell others exactly what I did for a career. I had trouble explaining what flower essences were, let alone family constellations. As I shifted from my old reality to a new one, change happened incrementally—I had to be patient.

Despite stepping off a conventional career track, there was still another layer of beliefs I had bought into: to be on a never-ending hamster wheel of busyness in order to feel productive and worthwhile—volunteerism, mothering, errands, and other activities that felt important and useful. Yet, the more I became aware of the forces acting on me, the more I saw how I could shift my perspective and slow the wheel. I could see the beliefs that were keeping me locked, and I could start to choose what I wanted to do and how I wanted to spend my time. I began to ask myself questions: Was I doing something because it was what others expected of me, or was it something I wanted to do for myself? Was I judging myself based on other people's expectations? Did I have healthy boundaries?

For short periods of time, I felt like I was waking up out of an almost unconscious state. If I could understand the stories that had shaped me, I felt that I could choose to step off the wheel and be loyal to my soul while at the same time, honor my family and my heritage. However, in every choice, there was the risk of rejection, particularly if I followed my own path. It is the way in which our soul, like a caged bird, calls to be set free, but part of letting your soul free is finding the courage to fly.

Questions help start the journey to seeing possibility, reclaiming your power, and leaving victimhood behind. They hold the key to the insights or answers you seek. It's easy to say what you don't want—an awful relationship, an unrewarding and dead-end job, and so on—and much harder to say what you *do* want. What is left if all that you dislike fell away? Questions, whether they are those that you are asked or those you ask yourself, can keep you moving forward instead of falling back into fear, opening you to receiving insights. The exercises at the end of this chapter pose some questions you might find helpful.

If you want something to change, you have to change your perception of it. My own experience taught me that if you can accept your reality—no matter how uncomfortable it is—you will eventually develop the insight that shifts it. Then your observed reality also changes because you are no longer in opposition to it. Only then can you open the doors to creative possibility—and yourself to transformation.

As you start to observe and learn, you build self-worth as you look back at your ability to handle challenges, build resilience, show up for yourself in little ways, and work with your ancestral stories. The more you can be in a relationship with yourself, the more you can see yourself with love and your history with coherence. On this journey, you will learn to honor your needs, dreams, and desires, and treat yourself with compassion. In the presence of your history and your life circumstances, your greatest support, strength, and trust will come from within, guiding and moving you forward. This will come from being aware of the choices you have in front of you and having confidence that you will base your decisions on the values that guide your life. Once you put your stake in the ground, synchronicities will start to show you the path so that you are in alignment with your soul and the Universe. You may doubt yourself, and you will be challenged, but if you persist, your faith in yourself and the Universe will be deepened.

## Self-Care and Self-Compassion

The earth is an emotional and karmic plane. The struggle of feeling unworthy and unlovable is the emotional challenge of being human. It stems from that deep need to be accepted as yourself, stripped of a résumé of accomplishments and achievements or the lack of them. According to psychologist Abraham Maslow, the desire to belong is a primal need. Yet so often, you feel like an outsider. The pressure to conform can cause you to ignore your feelings. To belong is to repress that part of you that sees things differently, constantly creating a battle between your impulse to individuate and the opposite one, to adhere to a group's expectations. Nowhere is this conflict more evident than in your relationships—family or otherwise. This challenge manifests itself as anger, frustration, hopelessness, anxiety, and self-doubt, ultimately putting a ceiling on your potential.

So, how do you honor your dreams, desires, aspirations, your feelings, and the need to individuate while belonging at the same time? When you feel hurt by someone's words or actions, it may be helpful to ask yourself the question, "What is the hole or emptiness inside of me that triggers this reaction within me?" Hidden wounds are like frozen ice within you that start to crack as perceived threats come close. But, by observing your reactions without judgment, acknowledging these feelings of inadequacy and your need for belonging and connection, you can see the shadows that you keep hidden from others and even yourself. Most often, it's an external search for validation and expectation that can never be filled by others. Instead, you can try to give these feelings of love, appreciation, acknowledgment, and support to yourself, treating yourself with kindness—especially when you are going through challenging circumstances. You could acknowledge what you are going through and compensate by giving yourself extra rest or just time to "do nothing."

When you hear a message from inside you about the void that you are trying to fill, you can try to release your automatically triggered reaction. The more you can take care of your feelings, the more you can accept yourself and give yourself the love and compassion you need. To be in nourishing relationship with others will depend on your ability to have a supportive relationship with yourself.

For instance, several studies have shown that although women are socialized to be caregivers to the members of their families—husbands, children, parents, friends, and communities—they really aren't taught to care for themselves. Research indicates that women tend to have slightly lower levels of self-compassion than men, even while they tend to be more caring, empathetic, and giving toward others. What you want to be able to do is balance being responsive to others with your own needs and feelings. If you don't see yourself as worthy, you will find it challenging to set boundaries and practice self-care. For children who have experienced physical or emotional abuse, or have very critical parents, self-compassion is often a struggle.

Two different studies looked at the behavior of self-compassionate individuals in their relationships as well as their resilience and optimism in the face of setbacks. One by Margaret Paul and Tasha Beretvas at the University of Texas, Austin, found that self-compassionate individuals were viewed as gentler and kinder by their partners. They were also able to give their partners more freedom and respected their partners opinions, and their relationships, in general, were more secure and satisfying. On the other hand, self-critical partners tended to be more aggressive and controlling. The second study, by David Sbarra at the University of Arizona, showed that self-compassion also helped individuals adjust better to divorce.

As you can see, you are not the only one who benefits from self-compassion. Kristen Neff, author of the book *Self-Compassion,* has observed that self-compassion allows you to give yourself the support to meet many of your own needs directly, and then you can also give your partner and others the emotional support they need. When you allow yourself to be "enough," you can simultaneously silence your inner critic and allow others to be "enough" as well.

## Blessings to Blossom

A key emotion that can often prevent you from honoring and setting boundaries for yourself is guilt, preventing you from being compassionate to yourself. It has often been said that a mother is only as happy as her unhappiest child. This shows the interconnectedness of emotions in a family. As you saw in Chapter 7, unconscious loyalties to parental unhappiness, their unlived desires, their negative relationship patterns, unsupportive beliefs, lack of professional success, etc., can manifest as loyalty to the behaviors and emotions you carry. A son might feel guilty that he is more successful or not as successful as his father. Inherited wealth can sometimes also cause feelings of guilt if a parent had to work hard and sacrifice for it. If a mother struggled to make ends meet and had little time for personal relationships or self-care, a daughter can feel guilty taking time out for a massage, or a visit to the spa, or spending time with friends. Family constellations showed me how damaging guilt can be for a parent or child left behind by fleeing refugees, for example. Guilt can prevent you from taking care of yourself and practicing self-care.

The act of touching the feet of your elders in India that I described in Chapter 3 was a ritual that honored the need to separate while releasing the conscious or subconscious need for permission to individuate. Much of the deeper meaning of this ritual is lost in modern-day India. However, it is a way of asking for *blessings* rather than *permission* when you pursue your dreams or go against parental expectations, especially if the relationship is fraught with tension. Small mom-and-pop stores in India often have a photograph of their late founder, grand-parents, or parents hanging on the wall. If you arrive at a store in the late morning when they have just opened, you may notice that these photographs have fresh garlands, and perhaps some incense burning below. The founder of a popular and thriving restaurant in my neighborhood in India would ask his mother to touch the pots and pans that food would be cooked in for the day. This is a way of acknowledging the importance of ancestral blessings for the success of their business.

If you were to accept the underlying idea behind these rituals—of the need to individuate—you can ask for ancestral or parental blessings rather than permission. Adapt this ritual by lighting a candle before the photographs of your ancestors or parents, asking for their blessings for your life. It doesn't matter if your parents or grandparents are dead or alive, but receiving blessings, even energetically, instead of subconsciously wanting or waiting for permission, helps you release buried guilt and allows you to move forward. It can also release unconscious loyalties that might be holding you back from living up to your potential.

You can then see yourself as worthy of achieving your dreams, receiving love, and having healthy relationships with others. You also start to see how other people project what they want onto you, and you can set healthy boundaries that allow you to take care of yourself. The more you choose actions that support you, the more you will find yourself worthy of your own love and self-acceptance.

# Filling the Hole Within

Your capacity to hold the challenges life presents you with keeps increasing as you do the work of acknowledging all who belong in the family and of healing wounds and righting wrongs no matter how ancient their origins are. Working with your family energy field, you will realize that you are not alone. On the other hand, you might even come to a stage where you can no longer identify with prejudices and negative beliefs that are part of belonging to a family, race, political party, or culture. You may ultimately choose to simply belong to the human race while still honoring your ancestors. The real challenge is choosing not to be blind to the faults of your family or tribe, but rather to be able to accept and honor them for who they are and at the same time, honor yourself as well—to stand in the space of non-judgment, acceptance, and acknowledgment.

You are the blossom of your family tree. And, just as flowers bloom in all kinds of conditions—arid deserts, at the edge of tumbling waterfalls, after devastating brushfires, in cracks in the sidewalk—you too can bloom just about anywhere. However, this process is a journey and does not happen overnight. I found that I needed to learn reverence and compassion for the vast canvas of life, and in order to create positive relationships, I had to connect to my ancestors and my heritage. Your lineage lives within you; when you have accepted your history and your own life circumstances, you will feel more authentic and complete. There will be a coherence within you and in your relationship with the world. Coming home to your roots and to yourself will give you the power you need to create the life you want. When you belong to yourself, you can find your place in the world and appreciate your shared humanity and the web of relationships that can fulfill and nurture you.

The feelings associated with *samadhi*, the blissful state of the yogis, are peace, harmony, contentment, love, gratitude, joy, and a consciousness of unity—your interconnection with the world and with others. It's interesting that we are often taught to search for happiness, not joy or bliss, because I don't know if I ever heard *samadhi* being described as "happy." The idea that at some point in my life, I would learn that magical formula that would allow me to be eternally happy is likely an illusion. However, emotions of joy, gratitude, peace, kindness, and contentment appear more often in my life now. I can see connections that I did not see before, and I allow these stories to land within me with compassion and awareness; this allows me to enter into life and the network of human relationships with an open heart. I am grateful for the gift of my life.

## Journal Exercises

1. Through family constellation therapy, I learned one key question to ask yourself when faced with issues or choices:

   *What is asking to be seen?*

   Namely, what laws of the family energy field have been violated and what feelings, or individuals, need to be acknowledged, remembered, or honored in order for healing to be possible?

   Often, when I ask myself this question, I find that there are related questions that can help to guide you. These are reflective and clarifying questions that might provide you with some insight into your situation, such as:

   *What do I need to be willing to see?*
   *What do I need to be willing to do differently?*

*What do I need to be willing to understand?*
*What do I need to be willing to learn in this situation?*
*What might I be resisting in this situation?*

If you are struggling with a particular situation, I invite you to ponder and write the answers to these questions in your journal. You can even write a question on a slip of paper and place it on your altar; you might be surprised at the insights you receive. When you search for answers, you open the door to allow trapped energy to leave the family system.

2. Do you tend to overrate criticism and underrate praise? Are you able to be kind to yourself, to nurture yourself? When you practice self-care, do you feel guilty and unworthy of the attention you're giving yourself? To open yourself to receiving, start noticing the ways in which you may be blocking it. "Sit" with the emotional discomfort while you relearn that it's okay to receive. Write down the ways in which you receive encouragement, support, and positive feedback—either in your journal or store the comments in a beautiful little box somewhere visible, like on your desk, bedside table, or vanity. If you receive a compliment, accept it without deflecting it or reciprocating. Simply say thank you. Identify your emotions if you can, or simply breathe as you notice the discomfort after such an incident. The journey to being open to receiving starts with these little changes.

   You might even notice whether you hold back genuine praise, encouragement, support, and appreciation of others. Do you tend to criticize other people's ideas?

   Perhaps you can even make a list of the things you appreciate about yourself—your physical features, your disposition, your strengths, your character, your achievements, your attitude, your talents, your skills, and the way in which you do things for others. Your list is limited only by your imagination. Add to it regularly, and look at it often or even daily as you start this process.

3.  To feel worthy of love and affection, consider using the flower essences suggested in this chapter. Choose one essence and journal how you feel about yourself over a three-week period, or combine some of them, depending on which ones resonate with you.

## A Mind Map Exercise

Often insights come unexpectedly like a whisper in the wind. You may have to train yourself to search for and receive insight into your situation. The exercise below is a tool that can help you capture the thinking that goes on inside your head, representing associations and connections with objects in order to get insight into a situation. These may be crystals, feathers, stones, or any other objects that catch your fancy that might be lying around the house.

Set aside a little space of time to do this exercise. If you'd like to, you can light a candle or play some soft music to relax and help you open your mind. You can even do it out in nature using objects like acorns, dried leaves, or little stones.

Begin by thinking of the issue you are struggling with. See if you can formulate the question that you are dealing with and perhaps your intention for the outcome you want. Trust that there are no right or wrong questions. The question that presents itself is the question that is uppermost in your mind. On any flat surface, or a piece of cloth on the floor, or the floor itself, you are going to place objects to represent yourself, the emotions of the issue—such as sadness, anger, etc.—and the events, people, and circumstances.

First, place an object for yourself and another object for the intention you have or the outcome you want. See where these two objects are in relation to each other. Notice how far or near they are to each other. Next, consider the challenge you are dealing with. Is it a person? An emotion? Place that where you feel it belongs. What other objects do you need to throw light on your situation? Add a representation for each of the emotions you feel and more for other people affecting the situation. How about your mother, father, grandparents, partner, or boss? Add these objects one at a time, slowly and deliberately, one by one. Observe any information you are receiving about the problem you are facing. Each time you add an object, keep checking in by picking up the object that you are using to represent yourself. What information do you get? You might choose to write down any insights. Work instinctively, intuitively trusting that you are placing the objects in the right places, at the right distance, and choosing the right objects for each representation. There is no right or wrong way to do this. Write the names of these emotions, beliefs, people, or events on little sticky notes or pieces of paper if you feel that you need to remember what each object is representing.

As you add objects to your physical mind map, do you need to move objects that you had placed earlier? You might even go back to picking up your original objects and moving them as you add new objects. It's possible some objects might move closer, some farther away. Notice the symbolism of the objects you have chosen. For example, perhaps you have chosen a timer to represent a relationship. What could that signify?

Look at associations between these objects you are representing, perhaps seeing what you might have missed before. Do you need thread, a string or beads, keychains, or something else that allows you to connect different objects together?

What outcome would you like? Are there objects that represent people or emotions that could lead to a creative outcome or possibility that does not currently exist in this scenario? Place those in there. See where they lie. What are they connected to? Write down your insights so that you can refer to them later.

You can leave your "mind map" out for a few days to come back to as you have time, and then remove it once you feel you have gained insight. You can burn some sage over the objects to "clear" them so that they are ready for use for another time.

## Flower Essences

**Walnut**—gives you strength to break away from the limiting influence of past experiences and strong personalities, helping you in making changes by giving you courage to follow the call of your destiny.

**Wild Oat**—Clarity and direction come from our inner realm, not the outer world. Wild Oat is the flower essence for when you are uncertain of your path forward and don't know what you should be doing. It gives you inner guidance.

**Oak**—helps you find your limits and open yourself to receiving help.

**Pine**—gives you inner self-esteem and self-acceptance. Feelings of guilt can be disproportionate to what has happened in the past or what you feel you need to do and cannot say no to. These feelings could be the result of your childhood or religious upbringing. But, with Pine you can let them go!

## A Self-Love and Self-Worth Formula

Fill a 30 mL dosage bottle that has a dropper with spring water and a teaspoon of brandy. If you want to create an alcohol-free formula, use glycerin as a preservative. Add two drops of each of the following essences.

**Crab Apple**—if you're self-critical, it helps you fall in love with yourself and let go of feelings of shame.

**Buttercup**—allows you to believe in your light and shine it out, without wondering if it's bright enough or big enough.

**Larch**—frees you from self-doubt and self-censure because you may feel that you are not up to the task and lack adequate training or capability. It allows you to believe in yourself, take a risk, and try something different or new. It helps build self-esteem.

**Wild Oat**—helps give you inner guidance and create steps toward success.

**Mimulus**—gives you courage to face your fears, reduces your anxiety, and helps you overcome shyness. Combined with the other essences, it also gives you courage to speak your truth.

**Pink Monkeyflower**—heals a deep sense of shame, guilt, and unworthiness, giving you the courage to reach out and take the emotional risk of being seen and allowing you to be in relationships with others.

**Calla Lily**— brings clarity about sexual identity, creates sexual self-acceptance, and helps integrate male and female qualities in a harmonious expression. If you feel you need this, you can add two drops to your formula.

*See Glossary for details about these essences.*

— THIRTEEN —

# The Four Pillars

There are four pillars that support the sacred center or sanctuary within you—your ancestors, the earth, your faith, and yourself. The actions that you take to honor your lineage, to connect with the earth, to take responsibility for yourself, and to deepen your faith keep the fire of this sanctuary burning. Working with these four pillars allows you to shift the way the past lives within you and be present to possibility. You can release anxiety and fear about the future and create the life you want.

I have watched family constellations with participants from different parts of the world, faiths, sexual orientations, and across genders. It is fascinating to me that irrespective of religion, the family energy field is always searching for healing. The toll exacted for breaking the principles of the family energy field is the same across the entire human race and the movement to harmony is through respect, gratitude, compassion, and understanding. The origin of tragedy lies somewhere in the past, its energy embedded in your family's energy field. For reasons you may never know, terrible things happened, and *being human* means that you too are not exempt. The pain of such deep tragedies may never leave you. In the face of sadness, grief, and horror inflicted by the family energy field as it seeks to make its presence felt, where does hope and healing lie?

All suffering contains within itself possible seeds of awareness and growth. Your personal pain may awaken you to a point
of transformation that leads to a disintegration of past patterns
and sets you on a journey that transforms not just your family
energy field, but the world around you. Once, I found myself
asking the question, "How much grief can our hearts hold?"
And the answer came back swiftly as if on the wings of angels:
"As much as is needed for our hearts to learn compassion." The
experience of grief is part of our shared humanity. And although
at some level you will always hold it, in the metamorphosis of
that grief is the doorway to compassion for the suffering of others. At some point, a pinhole of light may pierce the shroud of
darkness that surrounds you, and you may start not to ask "why"
but instead, "what now?" Through this process, you start to shift
invisible beliefs and behaviors that have kept you locked into
unconscious loyalty to your family system.

## The Price of Belonging

The family energy field is a powerful force field. Belonging to the
family system is like walking at the edge of a sheer precipice. You
are always balancing the right and wrong that has been done *to*
and *by* members of its system. Just as you pay a price for exclud-
ing others, you also pay a price for belonging. The price you pay
for belonging is identifying closely with the values and beliefs of
that family—money, relationships, education, work, or the roles
of men and women. You may also adopt negative beliefs about
other ethnic, religious, or racial minorities so that you remain
unconsciously allied with the family system.

You make your way through the safety of the womb into the
world in which you have arrived and with which you are expected

to conform. Knowingly or unknowingly, your life is influenced, if not governed by, the heritage you come from and the social and cultural *container* in which you live your life. Just like the family norms you believe in, you subscribe to social, political, and economic norms as well. You may be so unconsciously loyal to these beliefs that you participate in acts of exclusion, and even violence, toward others in order to stay part of your family system. Therefore, what is considered moral or ethical behavior may contradict this "tribal" loyalty, and you end up harming others, violating trust and respect. The most extreme forms of such acts are genocide or other violence toward another group. Although deeply morally reprehensible, participation in these crimes of hate and violence toward others can make people feel more like they belong to their "tribe." Some may even join other tribes, such as gangs or radical groups, if they are unconsciously drawn to the *idea of belonging* or if this is expected out of loyalty to their family system.

You may also jump through hoops or over hurdles that are set for you by society. Some of us might be more successful at it than others, but at some point in our lives, we might question how we have limited ourselves. You may then start to see how your culture has subconsciously shaped you and may have even caused you to lose sight of who you are and what you really want.

When you shift your sight to perception and insight, you can step away from the unconscious loyalties you hold—the beliefs and behaviors that do not allow you to be true to yourself—and hear the call of your soul. When you question what you thought felt safe and familiar, your world will expand. Although it can be a daunting journey, you can now start to become what you are capable of becoming. This liminal space of change is particularly challenging because you may not be able to see the path ahead and need to trust.

The journey from sight to insight was a long one for me, and it hasn't ended—it probably never will. I wish I could say that I never hit turbulent weather, storms, or other challenges. Yet lightning still strikes, and then I know that I have something more to learn. The lows are not as low and do not last as long, and deep within me, with certainty, I know that at some point the storm will pass, the sun will shine, and soft winds will continue to lift me higher. Asking questions, learning, healing, and growing are continuous, ever-expanding circles that allow me to step further into my power and answer the call of my destiny.

If you were to go against the opinion of your family or tribe and follow your dreams, you might be excluded from the group—an extremely painful experience. The fear of breaking these relationships and being abandoned by your family is so powerful that it keeps many tethered to the status quo. Think of children struggling to follow very different professional choices, express their sexual preferences or gender identities, or failing to live up to parental expectations. They are often racked with guilt or shame by the tension between their perceived individual and family or collective interest, between independence and interdependence.

Yet ultimately, by connecting to the flow of life and love from your parents, grandparents, and lineage, with its gifts and challenges, you start to hear the beat of the drum that echoes in your heart. I see people transformed as they work with their family energy fields. They see their family stories in a new light, and they see their unique purpose because they are releasing victimhood. As they shift, they expand their healing to help others. They start clinics and training programs in distant places, establish community gardens for healing in their towns, create workshops to help people tap into their inner genius, teach mindfulness, translate ancient Buddhist texts—the list is amazing, endless, and creative. A history of pillaging leads to caring for the earth; a history of atrocity toward another race leads to working with Indigenous people. There is something unconscious to this process. When you don't see yourself as a victim, you start to recover your self-worth, and you begin the journey to peace and harmony.

In order to heal myself and find my purpose, I had to honor all that I had disavowed in my culture and traditions. It took time for me to become proficient as a new practitioner of flower essences. It took me years to become settled in my work in healing. Huge life changes demand time, attention, and energy to overcome setbacks, rejection, and fear of failure. I often questioned what I was really doing, giving up a clearly defined job for something incomprehensible. But the changes that I saw emerge in my life centered and grounded me, and progress in the treatment of my clients was rewarding. My relationships blossomed. When I look back, I wonder if perhaps I am just a keeper of the spiritual flame passed down to me through the generations. Perhaps that is what I really came to America for: to rekindle that flame and to pass it on.

## The Path of Transformation

You draw to you not just your family energy field, but also different relationships—romantic partners, friends, colleagues—to help you heal and create transformation. From the most casual encounter to the intimate relationships you enter, all relationships have spiritual value: they awaken you to your blind spots and reveal the shadows you need to heal, forcing you to face what still needs work. You can choose to *see* and decide to walk a healing path as a result.

When you feel like a victim, you only see the patterns and behavior that other people or circumstances impose upon you; seldom do you see the emotional and behavioral patterns you yourself repeat again and again. In situations where you feel like a victim, you might ask yourself disempowering questions, such as "Why does this always happen to me?" You might even search for amends from those you feel wronged you—"When will they see what they have done and apologize?" These kinds of questions can cause you to feel stuck, unable to imagine the possibility of something different you could create for yourself. The victim routine runs deep. When you hold a view so deeply that you fail to see creative possibility, it's like having fault lines running through your sight. You know the saying "love is blind" or going "blind with rage." Patterns will continue to repeat in your life until you can see the hidden message behind them. In my life, I have always disliked uncertainty: moving continents, cities, and careers has been disconcerting and disorienting. This was not the life I had planned for myself, and I couldn't separate my own desires from the reality of my life. The illusion I carried was that my life *had* to be a certain way for me to be happy and I was not to blame for the circumstances of my life.

Yet, by being willing to admit that there are dragons within you, you can start paying attention to your feelings and emotions or to the physical cues your body is sending you. That's when you can begin releasing old emotional pain.

The breakthrough comes when you either start, or are forced by circumstances, to question the system, pattern, or environment you feel you're trapped in. It is then that you may find insight into your situation. It takes courage to accept reality, however uncomfortable it might be, rather than live with the comfort of an illusion you have held for a long time. I've learned, though, that this process of change, however painful, causes the shift from being a victim to becoming an observer and finally the creator of your life. The process repeats endlessly and is actually the presence of grace in your life.

## Connecting to the Flow of Love and Life

The ultimate challenge is to be grateful for your life and to receive and express love regardless of what life presents. Your outer journey, including the karmic patterns you inherit, can be viewed as a force that pushes you inward to heal your emotional patterns. As I discussed in Chapter 5, working with the flower essences has often been likened to "peeling an onion." The outermost layers of emotion are treated first and once you "peel" these layers, then you move to more deeply rooted issues. Just as emotions peel away to reveal deeper layers underneath, similarly, transgenerational patterns keep coming to the light of day to be released. Each time this happens, it gives you a chance to understand the origination of the emotional pattern and see how it affects the family system.

When the scales fall from your eyes and you can suddenly "see" what you didn't before, it can cause a lot of anguish and pain because the truth can be painful. When the ideas you've held for so long are challenged, and you are forced to see reality as it is, it is a call to expand your field of vision. This is because, as Jerry Kantor writes in *Interpreting Chronic Illness*, your eyes interpret "the chaos of light into brilliant, creative, and meaningful images," allowing you to become an active participant in your life rather than a passive victim.

It is this shift in perception that allows you to move from reaction to response instead of automatically reacting to triggers. This shift creates the possibility of choosing a new way of being and also rewriting the story you hold. As you learn the lesson, or "get the message," of the pattern that triggers the emotion, your field of vision expands toward insight, awareness, gratitude, compassion, and understanding. This is the spiritual aspect of healing. And ultimately, when you listen to the message of the emotions within you, acknowledge and remember your ancestors and honor yourself, your life shifts in a positive way.

Although other patterns will start to reveal themselves, your capacity to hold them and create change increases. In order to feel fully alive, you need to experience both negative and positive emotions. If you keep trying to avoid situations that cause you emotional pain, you limit your life experiences.

Forgiveness, gratitude, and compassion can be thought of as the *meta* or umbrella emotions that generate feelings of peace, contentment, and harmony. As you hold that compassion for others, there is a tremendous softening and opening of the heart. You do become gentler and kinder—including to yourself. Many great teachers have said if you cannot love yourself, you cannot love others. At the heart of healing heartbreak and grief and loving yourself is taking care of your emotions and learning self-compassion. Just as it's not easy to have compassion for others, it's also hard to have compassion for yourself. It is a struggle to be human. To be human is to be imperfect, but if you are able to release guilt, shame, anger, or bitterness and find self-compassion, you open the door to loving and accepting yourself. This process allows you to see beyond your unconscious loyalty to your family energy field, and to treat yourself and your relationships with respect. In the absence of this perception, you may be bound by loyalty to violent or negative behaviors, what-ever their roots might be, or even a repetition of family patterns tying you to your family of origin.

## From Sight to Insight

When you come to the point where you see what needs healing in yourself and address it, you are helping every member of your present family as well as those who have gone before you. When you make a place in your heart for everyone who belongs in the family, the healing you do and the love and grace you extend reverberates. Who should you make a place for? Not just the uncle who gets drunk and becomes rude at parties, the woman who "married in" and is disliked by everyone—the second wife, or the ne'er-do-well cousin that you exclude in your heart—these are the obvious ones. You also make room for those you unin-tentionally exclude—those who have harmed you and those you have harmed. While you are affected by the energy of your fam-ily system, you are never powerless.

*That's when the real healing happens.*

As you finish reading this book, you stand at the leading edge of your lineage, on the cusp of all that is possible, given your family history. You are born to bring your unique gifts into the world through the lineage that shapes you. There is a hole or void in the world that only you can fill when you have claimed yourself. Many may leave this world burdened by their family stories, never moving beyond them. But you have the oppor-tunity now to accept and allow all the pieces of your lineage to be part of you so you can grow beyond it and have compassion for the human race. Your ancestors can help you transform the burden of your stories and claim your destiny.

# Appendices

# APPENDIX A

# Some FAQs on Flower Essences

**How do I create my flower essence bottle?**

Fill a 30 mL dosage bottle that has a dropper with spring water and a teaspoon of brandy. If you want to create an alcohol-free formula, use glycerin as a preservative. Add two drops of each of the essences you want, using no more than seven at a time.

**Can I use flower essences without creating a customized dosage bottle?**

Yes, you can. Just add two drops of any essence to an 8-10 oz glass of water, or any other liquid, or put two drops directly in your mouth (although I find that if I take it directly, the taste is too strong for me). If you are using either the Five Flower Formula or Rescue Remedy, add four drops. For best results, you will want to sip it at about five-minute intervals for an hour or through the day. Since a customized dosage bottle lasts just over three weeks, if you are adding two drops to your liquid of choice, you may want to do this for a period of time (days or weeks) until you can feel the shift within you.

### How many times daily do I take my personalized essence?

If you make your own customized blend, it will be in what we call a dosage bottle with a dropper. Take four drops, four times daily—the first time when you awake, the last time when you go to bed, and twice in between.

### How should I take the essence?

You can take each dosage directly from the bottle with the dropper, but be careful: don't let the dropper touch your mouth. This could contaminate the infusion. You can also carefully add the drops to any liquid, such as tea, coffee, juice, water, or even soup.

### Is there a preservative in the infusion?

Flower essence practitioners mix your personalized flower essence with pure spring water and put it into the dosage bottle. We add a teaspoon of brandy as a preservative to prevent the water from spoiling. If you prefer not to have alcohol in your dosage, let your practitioner know. They will add vegetable glycerin as a preservative to the pure spring water. If you are making your own bottle, you can add either alcohol or glycerin.

### How do I store my infusion?

Please keep the bottle away from direct sunlight. If you can, keep it away from computers and cell phones.

### Can I take flower essences with other medications?

If you are taking prescribed medications for physical or emotional ailments, you can usually take flower essences. The essences are vibrational in nature and are chosen on the basis of mental and emotional issues rather than physical conditions. They are not intended to deal with serious mental or emotional conditions or a known physical medical problem. For these, you would seek the care or advice of a qualified health practitioner. If you are on medications, it is always prudent to consult your doctor, who can monitor your physical condition. And please, never discontinue medication without medical supervision.

### How do I know my flower essence is working?

Each flower essence works subtly and gently, so you probably won't perceive a quick emotional difference. But in two to three weeks, clients generally feel calmer, less tired, and more centered. At this time, many people also experience noticeable positive changes in their behavioral responses to once-bothersome events. They realize their emotional health is improving.

### How long do I take these essences?

This answer depends on you. By the end of three consultations, some clients feel they have adequately overcome their emotional challenges. But emotions are like onions: they have multiple layers of skin. As we peel away the outermost layers, we move closer to the core and discover previously undisclosed emotional issues. Each personalized blend of flower essences will continue to work at these deeper levels. So how long you take a particular essence is ultimately up to you. How deep do you want to explore? Your flower essence will provide you with emotional support; it will empower you.

# Flower Essences and Essential Oils

What are the differences between flower essences and essential oils? Here is a look at some of the features for a better understanding.

**Amount that is needed**

Usually, a large number of flowers are needed to create essential oils. For instance, it takes ten thousand roses to create 5 mL or about a teaspoon of essential oil.

Flower essences, on the other hand, are made with a few flowers in a bowl of water. The water carries the energetic imprint of the flower, and we can get several bottles of flower essences from those few flowers.

**Internal versus external**

Essential oils are not taken internally, and unless they are food-grade essential oils, they can be toxic to the system. Even a topical application requires essential oils to be diluted with a carrier oil.

Flower essences, on the other hand, are taken internally and are completely gentle and safe even for children and pets. They have no side effects.

## Scented versus unscented

Essential oils, as the name suggests, are oils extracted from the stem, leaves, or other parts of the plant through steam distillation or other methods and carry a smell or fragrance. Through the ages, they have often been used in perfumes.

Flower essences have no smell since they are made from the energetic imprint of the flower. Wildflowers are picked and floated in a crystal or glass bowl filled with water placed on a rock or the earth in the early morning sun. After a few hours, the flowers are removed, and the water is strained and preserved with brandy. So, flower essences are wildflower infusions in water.

## How they work

Essential oils are often used to address physical symptoms and provide overall stress relief through the diffusion of their smell. They work through the olfactory system and the associated regions of the brain that govern our stress response.

Flower essences target specific emotions and the thoughts that are connected to those emotions. They work at the energetic level. For instance, your judgments can overwhelm you: the "shoulds," the "musts," the "have-tos," and all kinds of judgments about yourself, others, situations, and events. Flower essences shift these thoughts and provide calmness, clarity, and direction and give us inner confidence.

# A Starter Kit of Flower Essences

To heal your roots and release the patterns that hold you back, I have put together these ten essences that could be used as a starter kit. While the thirty-eight Bach flower remedies are considered a complete system, I have listed here some remedies that seem to come up frequently in dealing with the issues I have discussed in the book. These are not all Bach flower remedies, and once you are familiar with the use of essences, you might want to explore others that may feel more appropriate for you. Detailed descriptions of each of these essences are in the Glossary below.

You could create a customized dosage bottle for yourself, adding two drops of each of these essences or simply use one at a time. Do not add more than seven at a time. I strongly encourage journaling while using the essences to help keep track of how they are helping you. However, if you are not up to it, don't berate yourself. The essences will still support you!

To this kit, I would recommend adding Rescue Remedy or, as it is sometimes called, the Five Flower Formula. It's always good to have on hand anytime you are stressed, anxious, or upset. It helps calm and center you. You might want to add four drops of it each time to the dosage bottle you make for additional support. And, yes, it does count as one of the maximum seven essences.

1. **Baby Blue Eyes**—helps you feel more confident, receptive to the world, trusting and accepting people around you. If you didn't have a strong positive connection with your father or a father figure, this essence can help.

2. **Beech**—for censoring your inner critic and becoming more tolerant and empathetic toward others.

3. **Chestnut Bud**—helps you understand the meaning behind the repetitive and habitual patterns that repeat in your life.

4. **Chicory**—releases patterns of clinginess, neediness, possessiveness, and manipulation that carry over from one generation to the next, from parents to children, but can be hard to see. Chicory creates calm inside as you let go of expectations and cease to struggle for validation, appreciation, gratitude, or acknowledgment. It promotes unconditional love.

5. **Holly**—for anger, suspicion, jealousy, envy, the feeling of betrayal, the desire for revenge—all the emotions that can keep us tightly in their grip, spiking whenever misunderstandings and the feeling of not being loved enter your life.

6. **Larch**—frees you from self-doubt, self-censure, and fear of taking a risk. Larch allows you to believe in yourself—it gives you that elusive self-esteem that can often be lost early in childhood.

7. **Mariposa Lily**—for when human mothering is inadequate; through this essence you can experience

the presence of the nurturing divine or archetypal mother energy.

8. **Pine**—gives you inner self-esteem and self-acceptance. Feelings of guilt can be disproportionate to what has happened in the past, causing you to feel that you need to do more than you should, or that you cannot say no. Pine gives you the inner ability to perceive the situation accurately. It helps you learn to nurture yourself instead of blaming yourself.

9. **Walnut**—gives you the strength to break away from the limiting influence of past experiences, constricting beliefs, and outmoded values of a community. This essence can help by disrupting the control by a dominant or forceful personality. It is invaluable for all life transitions by helping you to make changes—giving you the courage to follow the call of your destiny or to end or begin relationships. This strength can help you make career changes or pursue your dreams.

10. **Willow**—helps you let go of resentment when you are filled with bitterness and negativity. Willow helps you take responsibility for yourself, let go of victimhood, and gives rise to feelings of forgiveness, including of yourself, and finding gratitude for life.

# APPENDIX D

# Five Flower Essence Formulas

Most flower essence practitioners do not recommend formulaic approaches because they may not address deep-seated issues. The beauty and strength of the flower essence remedies lie in their customization. However, I have listed some formulas here that can help address the issues that I discuss in the book based on the emotions I have observed coming up frequently.

## Formula #1: An Optimism Formula

Fill a 30 mL dosage bottle that has a dropper with spring water and a teaspoon of brandy. If you want to create an alcohol-free formula, use glycerin as a preservative. Add two drops of each of the following essences.

**Gorse:** This essence lifts the hopelessness of the moment and restores faith and a positive outlook.

**Gentian:** When a setback feels like a mountain, Gentian brings it back to a molehill, helping you feel that you are up to the challenge.

**Sweet Chestnut:** When you feel you have reached your breaking point, feel alone, and your anguish feels unbearable, bottomless, and endless, Sweet Chestnut lifts the burden of this suffering.

**Elm:** This flower essence creates the capacity so that you are not overwhelmed by it all. It restores confidence in your abilities when you feel unequal to the challenge. It allows you to open yourself to receiving help as well.

**Mustard:** This flower essence takes you through the darkness and restores emotional balance.

**Heather:** When you are absorbed in your pain and worries, you can feel deeply alone. This essence heals this feeling of profound emptiness within and shifts it by caring for and seeing the suffering of others as well. It brings a sense of strength within.

## Formula #2: Boundaries

Fill a 30 mL dosage bottle that has a dropper with spring water and a teaspoon of brandy. If you want to create an alcohol-free formula, use glycerin as a preservative. Add two drops of each of the following essences.

**Walnut:** This essence gives you the strength to pursue your dreams, end or begin relationships, and make career changes. It allows you to persevere despite the objections and ridicule of people around you.

**Pink Yarrow:** When you "give too much" and try to solve other peoples' problems, Pink Yarrow gives you the support you need, preventing you from becoming too much of an "empath."

**Centaury:** This essence releases the need to please others and to take care of others by ignoring or neglecting your own needs. Paradoxically, this kind of behavior can stunt the growth of those closest to us to whom we find it hard to say no.

**Pine:** Feelings of guilt can be disproportionate to what has happened in the past or what you feel you need to do and cannot say no to, but, with Pine, you can let them go!

**Chicory:** This essence can help bring you back to your center. When you feel a lack of attention and a need for appreciation, validation, and acknowledgment, it can help to release these feelings. It helps when you feel invisible!

**Red Chestnut:** Anxiety, concern, or even obsessive worry for your loved ones act as a drain on your relationships as well as on your mental peace as you constantly anticipate problems for your loved ones. Red Chestnut shifts this anxiety into trust in the capacity of those you love to deal with issues.

## Formula #3: Self-Love and Self-Worth

Fill a 30 mL dosage bottle that has a dropper with spring water and a teaspoon of brandy. If you want to create an alcohol-free formula, use glycerin as a preservative. Add two drops of each of the following essences.

**Crab Apple:** If you are self-critical, this essence can release shame and obsessiveness about the physical body. It can help restore a balanced relationship with your body, helping you let go of these feelings.

**Buttercup:** This essence allows you to believe in your light and shine, without wondering if it's bright enough or big enough. Buttercup helps your soul gather the strength to live according to its own code, moving beyond the standards of success imposed by the world.

**Larch:** This essence allows you to believe in yourself. I often combine Buttercup with Larch, the flower essence that frees you from self-doubt, self-censure, and the feelings of not being up to the task because of your abilities, skills, or training. With these two together, you can unlock *your* essence with confidence!

**Pink Monkeyflower:** Sometimes we carry a fear—a fear of others seeing our pain, the wounds of our past—which could be any form of abuse or other trauma. Pink Monkeyflower heals this deep sense of shame, guilt, and unworthiness, giving us the courage to take the emotional risk of being seen, which allows us to be in a relationship with others.

**Pine:** Feelings of guilt can be disproportionate to what has happened in the past or what you feel you need to do and cannot say no to. Pine restores your inner self-esteem and self-acceptance.

**Rock Water:** This essence releases energetic blocks in the body and the mind, especially if you have been holding yourself to very high standards manifesting in a push to be perfect. It helps you get in touch with feelings that might have been deeply buried.

**Calla Lily:** If you feel you need it, you can add two drops of Calla Lily. This essence brings clarity about sexual identity, allowing for sexual self-acceptance and helping to integrate male and female qualities in a harmonious expression of the self.

## Formula #4: Need Direction?

What kind of decision-maker are you? There are styles of decision-making. There are people who tend to vacillate between two choices, sort of like Macbeth—to do or not to do, and then there are others who have an instinctive response but tend to ask others what to do. In the end, they make a decision that they are not happy with later. Neither is a great option. Over the years, I've started to trust my own instincts and make decisions. As I have become more aware of my values and the factors that drive me, I can depend on myself more. I also find myself waiting for that voice to tell me what to do. In this grand mystery of life, we want to move toward that space that guides our choices and our decisions from a place of greater wisdom and compassion for what's best for us.

**Scleranthus:** Those who vacillate between two options need Scleranthus. And those who talk to others and end up not trusting themselves, following advice they later regret, need Cerato.

**Cerato:** The essence of this little blue flower allows you to trust your judgment, build your discernment, and connect with your inner guidance.

**Wild Oat:** If you are wondering what to do, add Wild Oat for direction. Clarify your ambitions, find your purpose, create specific steps for success: wouldn't you love to do that? Clarity and direction come from our inner realm, not the outer world, and Wild Oat essence brings inner clarity.

**Walnut:** This essence gives you the strength to break away from the limiting influence of past experiences, constricting beliefs, and outmoded values of a community. This essence can help by disrupting control by a dominant or forceful personality or family. Walnut is invaluable for all life transitions by helping you to make changes by giving you the courage to follow the call of your destiny or to end or begin relationships. This strength can help you pursue your dreams or make career changes.

**Wild Rose:** I often give my clients Wild Rose when I notice there is an apathy or disinterest in activities and in life. They seem resigned to their life and lack the will or effort to improve their circumstances, find joy, or access the passions they once had. You will find yourself doing things, but the shift is so subtle that it's easy to miss it.

**Mimulus:** This is the remedy that reduces anxiety and gives you courage to face your fears—including fear of failure, fear of success, and fear of being rejected or hurt.

## Formula #5: Letting Go

There are many emotions connected with grief and sadness. These may be underlying the anger or bitterness you feel. You might find that these essences may help you.

**Willow:** This essence helps when you have lost your belief in the fairness of life. The essence of Willow picks you up when you are drowning in self-pity and sorrow, allowing you to flow with all that life has to offer.

**Holly:** This is the essence to help calm anger, suspicion, jealousy, envy, the desire for revenge—all the emotions that separate us from feeling love and compassion toward others and keep us locked in negativity.

**Beech:** Harsh criticism and judgment of others come from having grown up or being in an environment that is extremely critical. These conditions lead us to cover our own sense of insecurity and inferiority by projecting it onto others. It reduces hypersensitivity to your personal and social environment.

**Chicory:** As you let go of expectations and cease to struggle for validation, appreciation, or acknowledgment, Chicory creates calm inside you. It brings a freedom that allows others to be free as well.

**Vine:** Control is a way in which we can deal with the constant change that life throws us. This essence releases the need for being in control, having your way, and knowing the right way to do it. It allows you to listen to other opinions and to guide others without needing to control or dominate.

**Bleeding Heart:** This essence helps us let those we love go. It transforms the pain so that we can understand how much our capacity to love others is also built on our capacity to nourish ourselves. We love more freely and unconditionally in letting go than holding on.

**Honeysuckle:** This striking red trumpet-shaped flower is a clarion call to the present, allowing you to draw your energies back from the past. Honeysuckle flower essence lets us let go of the past—the way it grips our heart in memories that either pull us back there or stop us from going where we need to go.

# Glossary

**Angel's Trumpet:** The white flower used to create this essence is long and trumpet-shaped, facing down toward the earth. Originally from South America, it emits a fragrance in the evening. It is an essence that helps the individual soul surrender to the spiritual world and even death, release the resistance of letting go, and support it in crossing the threshold between life and death. It is particularly helpful in situations where death is seen as fearful and terrifying, yet the soul is ready to depart the physical body. It transforms the fear of death into a "conscious awareness of spiritual life" (Kaminski & Katz, *Flower Essence Repertory*, 2004).

**Baby Blue Eyes:** If you didn't have a strong positive connection with your father or a father figure, this essence can help. A father may have been absent emotionally, physically, or may have been violent. The lack of feeling secure, safe, protected, or guided may show up in an inability to trust others, to feel that the world is safe, and a rupturing of a connection or trust with a higher power or spiritual world. While it can also lead to antisocial or criminal tendencies, the loss of fathering support can lead to defensiveness and cynicism as well. Baby Blue Eyes allows you to feel supported, loved, and more connected to a larger spiritual force. It also helps you to feel confident, receptive to the world, and trusting and accepting of the people around you. This essence also helps you respond with understanding and acceptance to male figures of authority.

**Beech:** We all often need a good dose of Beech. Criticism, intolerance, and judgment of others—at their habits, mannerisms, gestures, or idiosyncrasies—all point to the way in which we project expectations onto others instead of looking within and healing ourselves. Often, this harsh criticism and judgment of others come from having grown up or being in an environment that is extremely critical, leading us to cover our own sense of insecurity and inferiority by projecting it onto others. Beech helps you accept other people's imperfections and be more tolerant of them. By censoring your inner critic, it promotes empathy, helps you become less judgmental and more tolerant of others and to make allowances for their shortcomings.

**Buttercup:** Mother Teresa once said, "Not all of us can do great things. But we can do small things with great love." That, I learned, is the essence of Buttercup, a small and humble yellow flower that hides great power. Buttercup allows you to believe in your light and shine it out, without wondering if it's bright enough or big enough. Your soul gathers the strength to live according to its own code, moving beyond the standards of success imposed by the world, not needing external validation, filled with self-esteem.

**Calla Lily:** It brings clarity about sexual identity and creates sexual self-acceptance if you are struggling with sexual gender identity. This essence helps integrate and balance the male and female qualities at a deeper level—because, at some level, we all have both "masculine" and "feminine" characteristics within us. This essence releases a sense of confusion and creates self-acceptance and coherence within.

**Centaury:** If you find it hard to say no to others, this is the essence that helps you set boundaries. Constantly giving without taking care of our own needs depletes us and makes us resentful. Underlying the constant giving is a desire to keep others happy and please them, which leads to a sense of acknowledgment and validation. When we honor ourselves, we can also take care of others without feeling burdened, exhausted, and depleted. Centaury helps you to say no so that you can stop focusing on pleasing others and neglecting your own needs. It helps you to create a boundary and to be true to yourself so you are able to walk your own path while helping others. While habitually pleasing others, it can be hard to recognize your own needs. Paradoxically, this kind of behavior can stunt the growth of those closest to us whom we find it hard to say no to.

**Cerato:** The essence of this little blue flower allows you to trust your judgment, build your discernment, and find your opinions. It works well for those who talk to others about their decisions and end up not trusting themselves, following advice they later regret. This indecision and confusion can be draining and exhausting.

**Cherry Plum:** This essence is a response to the call for help from the depths of our soul in the face of severe ongoing physical or mental stress and strain. It is even for those who are in deep depression and despair leading them to contemplate suicide (though professional help must also be contacted in this case). When things are pressing on you so much and the tension is so great, you feel you might snap, have a nervous breakdown, lose control, or feel that you might become violent toward someone or even yourself. You might be losing your temper with frequent outbursts, be hysterical, or destructive, even throwing things, and are afraid of losing control. Despite extreme stress, this essence restores balance and brings back strength and a sense of stability, releasing the accompanying tension and fear.

**Chestnut Bud:** This essence helps free you from the repetitive and habitual patterns that repeat in your life. What are you resisting *seeing*? What are you resisting *learning*? What causes you to repeat the same experiences and same mistakes? Your soul is trying to speak to you. This is the essence that helps you learn the key lesson or lessons embedded in those experiences, releasing the karma that keeps you tied to those resistant patterns. It makes you observant, perceptive, and discerning, helping you understand the wisdom and knowledge of those past experiences. While Wild Oat (see Wild Oat later in this Glossary) gives you direction for the future, Chestnut Bud teaches you the lessons of the past. It's also a great essence for children in helping them learn.

**Chicory:** Patterns of clinginess, neediness, possessiveness, and manipulation carry over from one generation to the next, from parents to children, but can be hard to see. *Mother* and *smother* are only one letter apart. Yet, it's not just a mothering relationship that might need Chicory. I see it in relationship patterns between partners or spouses and in other relationships as well. It's hard to tell because this relationship is characterized by so much love and giving. But since human love is an imperfect offering, it can be suffocating as well, demanding, or needy, in overt and covert ways. In its covert form, people who need Chicory can almost seem like martyrs because of their *over-care*—believing that they know what is best for others and sharing those views with their loved ones. They do want their friends and family to be close, but paradoxically, can often criticize or interfere in the lives of their loved ones, pushing them away. This behavior can hide a deep need for validation, appreciation, and acknowledgment. When children need Chicory, we see behavior that pulls on the attention of others in a negative way such as tantrums, clinginess, fussiness, or neediness. Chicory helps us love while respecting the freedom and individuality of those we love. It teaches us to love. You might read this and say, "Oh, I know someone who really needs this, but they won't take it." Since we all carry the shadow of what we dislike within us, I would suggest you take this essence yourself. The call for Chicory essence is sometimes so subtle that it's almost easy to miss it. Chicory creates calm inside as you let go of expectations and cease to struggle for validation, appreciation, gratitude, or acknowledgment. It brings a freedom that allows others to be free as well. It brings unconditional love into our hearts.

**Crab Apple:** When we are obsessed with perfection—or rather the imperfections around us—in ourselves and our surroundings, we need Crab Apple. If there is a sense of shame about the physical body, Crab Apple can restore a balanced relationship with our body—helping us let go of these feelings. I would go further and say that it can make you fall in love with yourself *as you are*. When I see an obsessive need for cleanliness, it's the call for Crab Apple. Those who need Crab Apple are preoccupied with feeling unclean, perhaps even bathing several times a day, washing their hands continuously, or other ways in which they want to release the feelings of disgust and shame from their deepest core.

**Elm:** This essence is for when you feel overwhelmed. Do you feel up to the task at hand? Or do you feel inadequate, despondent, or exhausted by what you have to do? When feelings of doubt take over concerning all that you need to contend with, and you are having trouble facing all that you must accomplish, reach for this essence. It will open you up to receiving help from others—in itself a key strength. And it will also restore your faith and inner confidence in your ability to complete whatever you need to do, letting go of what is not vital. You might usually feel confident, but it's dealing with what's "on your plate" that can make you feel temporarily unequal to the task at hand.

**Gentian:** Combine Gorse with Gentian—one of my favorite essences—for self-doubt, setbacks, and discouragement. When a setback feels like a mountain, Gentian brings it back to a molehill. Pessimists often take longer to lift themselves up. Gentian will do some of the uphill work for you—helping you feel that you are up to the challenge and giving you the fortitude to discover solutions. It allows you to shift your perspective and become more persistent and therefore resilient. You will start to feel that no obstacle is too big to overcome.

**Gorse:** This essence is for hope—when things feel bleak and helpless. Hope is the hardest love we carry—for ourselves! It's hard work, keeping the flame of hope alive. Gorse is the flower essence that maintains hope when it is hard to see in the darkness, when you've been told that nothing more can be done, when you are convinced that you just inherited this condition or fate, and pessimism has free rein. Just like the tiny yellow flowers, Gorse lifts the hopelessness of the moment and restores faith and optimism, bringing with it a sunnier outlook. Gorse brings a luminous inner light to the darkest situation, helping us feel there is always light at the end of the proverbial tunnel no matter how dark the tunnel seems. Hope and faith in ourselves, in life, and the Universe.

**Grounding Green:** This essence is a true bouquet of green flowers—Green Rein Orchid, Green Bells of Ireland, Lady's Mantle, Green Rose, Green Cross Gentian, and Green Nicotiana—and food-grade essential oils—Silver Fir, Sitka Spruce, and Cedarwood. It is for building your connection to the earth, helping you become deeply aware of it and to be nourished by it. You will find yourself wanting to connect with the mother that nurtures you—Mother Earth herself—receiving her gifts with an open heart.

**Heather:** When you are absorbed in your pain and worries, you can feel deeply alone. This loneliness may make its presence felt by your need to talk to others, a dislike of being alone, and the feeling of being close to tears. This essence heals this profound feeling of inner emptiness and shifts it by giving strength from within, which leads to caring for and seeing the suffering of others.

**Holly:** It's probably no accident that Holly is associated with Christmas since it is the essence for compassion and love. I often park my car by a holly tree, and in the fading light, I hear lots of sparrows come home to nest in its branches as darkness settles. Invariably, we will need Holly essence for anger, suspicion, jealousy, envy, the desire for revenge—all the emotions that separate us from feeling love and compassion toward others. It's an essence I strongly recommend keeping at hand, and when you start to feel those feelings—and misunderstandings arise—reach for this essence. You will be surprised to see how they dissipate.

**Honeysuckle:** This essence lets us let go of the past—the way it grips our heart in memories that either pull us back there or stop us from going where we need to go. Sometimes making space for something different means physically making space. You might be surprised at what you start to let go of when you take this essence. Not only does it help with nostalgia, homesickness, and memories, but it also helps us let go of regret and be at peace with the present.

**Hornbeam:** Add two drops of Hornbeam if you have been procrastinating. I'm always surprised at what I might tackle on my to-do list with a little bit of Hornbeam! When your daily tasks seem burdensome and that constant Monday morning feeling wears you down, Hornbeam shifts your energy. Sometimes, you might discover as I did, it was not on my list, but on my mind!

**Impatiens:** The only flower essence so closely tied in name to what it does—it stops you from being irritable so that you can have patience with the larger timetable of life and appreciate the ephemerality of the present moment.

Impatiens will encourage you to have patience with the other drivers in traffic, the weather, the world. This essence helps you understand the subtleties of time by releasing the pressure of time and bringing you back into the present. People who need this essence tend to be always busy and prefer to work alone because they are impatient with the slowness of others. This makes them irritable as well. After taking this essence, they become more patient and tolerant with conditions that would frustrate or upset them.

**Joshua Tree:** To free ourselves from conditioning and awaken to compassion and healing is the journey of our soul. In the process, our soul can find its purpose and make choices. Joshua Tree flower essence helps us release hardened family patterns, offering us hope and lifting us to a higher consciousness. However, it is not usually an essence that is used at the start, but as an individual continues the journey with flower essences. It leads to centering, and an inner-directed life that gives you the strength to face adverse circumstances and relationships. It leads to deep healing at the soul level, so it's sometimes best to prepare yourself for the capacity to deal with such change with other essences first. Patricia Kaminski and Richard Katz of Flower Essence Services consider Joshua Tree flower essence to be a powerful healing catalyst in releasing the negative inheritance from our family and ethnic legacies.

**Larch:** I often combine Buttercup with Larch, the flower essence that frees you from self-doubt, self-censure, and fear of taking a risk. Larch allows you to believe in yourself—it gives you that elusive self-esteem that can often be lost early in childhood. It allows you to release the fear you project on a situation—of failing badly, of underperforming, of being judged harshly. These fears can often prevent you from even trying something new. Larch flower essence gives you the courage to take risks and just try, instead of holding yourself back! Larch gives you the inner confidence to express yourself freely and creatively. You can unlock that part of you—*your* essence—with confidence.

**Mariposa Lily:** Family trauma, abuse, abandonment, neglect, economic hardship, and even cultural factors can lead to a rupturing of a positive relationship with one's mother. It may have been hard for a multiplicity of reasons to have received unconditional maternal love. This essence helps you to come to terms with the pain of this past. When human mothering is inadequate, through this essence, you can experience the presence of the nurturing divine or archetypal mother energy. Mariposa lily grows from a bulb, buried deep underground, which gives it the ability to survive wildfires. Similarly, this essence allows you to feel that warm, loving maternal presence within you, despite having been burned by the mother wound. It brings balance to your energies of family and nurturing, breaking patterns of pain and neglect.

**Mimulus:** I observed the tiny yellow Mimulus growing near the clear, swiftly flowing stream in the Sierra Nevada. A small yellow flower that grows on the edge of fresh, flowing water, it looks like it clings precariously to life. Yet, belying that tenuous hold is fierce determination. If you can name your fear, it's usually Mimulus flower essence: fear of spiders, fear of flying, fear of public speaking. This is the remedy that brings courage to face those small everyday fears and is especially good for shyness, including shy children. Underneath these fears is a larger unconscious fear that can perhaps even be traced back to a "hesitation at the moment of incarnation" itself (Kaminski and Katz, *Flower Essence Repertory*, 2004). This essence gives you the courage to face your fears, reduce anxiety, and overcome shyness, including the big Fs: fear of failure, fear of success, and fear of being rejected or hurt.

**Mustard:** When I was young and driving to my grandmother's house in the wintertime, we would sometimes pass by fields of yellow mustard flowers. Even on a gloomy day, the yellow field was like an unexpected ray of sunshine. If you find yourself down in the dumps for no obvious reason, this is the essence to have on hand. It might seem as if the blues came on suddenly, unconnected to situations around you, but this might be because of past experiences that lie submerged in your subconscious memory. Mustard flower essence takes us through the darkness and restores our emotional balance.

**Oak:** The tree sacred to the Druids, the religious leaders of the ancient Celtics, was used to build ships and cathedrals. It was known for its strength and endurance. We often, even today, refer to the oak tree as mighty! Like the mighty oak, people who need this essence will serve others beyond the limits of their endurance. When this need to serve comes from a sense of duty and responsibility, not from an enjoyment of pleasing others, this can come at great personal cost and can lead to burnout. This essence helps you find your limits and open yourself to *receiving* help.

**Pine:** Do you feel guilty when you say no? Do you feel you are letting people down? Do you reproach yourself? This is the essence for the guilt complex that robs us of joy. One of the challenges in setting boundaries is the feeling of guilt. Pine gives you inner self-esteem, self-acceptance, and self-approval. Feelings of guilt can be disproportionate to what has happened in the past or what you feel you need to do and cannot say no to. These feelings of self-blame could be the result of your childhood or religious upbringing, but, with Pine essence, you can let them go!

**Pink Monkeyflower:** There are several monkeyflowers that heal different emotional response patterns. Monkeyflowers, so called because they resemble a monkey's face, are almost like a mask we might wear. Sometimes we carry a fear of others seeing our pain, the wounds of our past—which could be any form of abuse or trauma or a similar kind of experience. We want to hide this pain from the world—the sense of shame, the fear of being "found out" in some way, and then rejected. Pink Monkeyflower heals this deep sense of shame, guilt, and unworthiness, giving us the courage to reach out and take the emotional risk of being seen and allowing us to be in relationships with others.

**Pink Yarrow:** This essence prevents you from taking on other people's emotions and becoming too much of an "empath." It helps you be compassionate without merging with another person's emotions completely. It is particularly helpful for highly sensitive souls, to help them be compassionate while keeping their own emotional boundaries. When you "give too much" and try to solve other people's problems, Pink Yarrow gives you the support you need to be helpful and compassionate without absorbing their emotions.

**Pomegranate:** I have always been fascinated by the story of Persephone, who was abducted by Hades to his underworld. Each year in autumn, she is compelled to return because she ate the pomegranate seeds while dwelling there. In spring, she returns to flowering Mother Earth. Juggling literally between worlds, trying to find that balance between home, family, and the creative self—this essence helps people find balance and to understand and see their choices and, ultimately, to find fulfillment and joy.

**Post-trauma Stabilizer:** This combination of heart-centered flower essences—Arnica, Bleeding Heart, Echinacea, Glassy Hyacinth, Green Cross Gentian, Fireweed, and the Five Flower Formula—helps you recover from the depths of sorrow, despair, and defeat, allowing you to find hope, relief, connection, healing, and vitality. This blend helps if recurring dreams and memories of past trauma keep resurfacing or recurring. It also helps deal with the shock or numbness from disasters, especially if you lost your home or community—even if it was a long time ago. If you have shut out your emotions, it can bring them to the surface so that they can be processed and released. While it is a beautiful blend of soothing essences, it does have a strong alcohol taste owing to the brandy used as a preservative. You can spray it around you or add it to a base cream, stir it, and massage yourself with it. I usually add four sprays into a dosage bottle.

**Red Chestnut:** Think of your child wanting to share something with you but hesitating because they are worried about causing you concern, that your caretaking will shift from support for them to anxiety. This kind of anxiety, concern, or even obsessive worry for your loved ones acts as a drain on your relationships as well as on your mental peace as you constantly anticipate problems for your loved ones. Red Chestnut shifts this anxiety into trust in the greater unfolding of life, helping you believe in the capacity of those you love to deal with issues on their own.

**Rescue Remedy:** This popular combination of five flower essences (Rock Rose, Cherry Plum, Star of Bethlehem, Impatiens, and Clematis) is used even by several movie stars. Rescue Remedy supports you and gives you temporary relief, but it does not provide deep healing. It helps when you receive unexpected bad news, have a car accident, or have an argument with someone. Put four drops in an 8-10 oz glass of water or in a bottle of water and sip it. Initially take it every three to five minutes for an hour, and then as often as you like until you feel better.

**Rock Rose:** The key word that describes the need for this essence is *terror*. Whenever there is terror or panic in you or around you, this is the essence to reach for. Add a few drops in a little water and sip it frequently. It will help you find courage in these extreme circumstances and become calmer. It is one of the key essences in Rescue Remedy, also known as the Five Flower Formula.

**Rock Water:** This essence was the only remedy Dr. Bach created that was not from a flower but from an underground spring. It contained the essence of water—flow. Rock Water releases energetic blocks in the body and the mind. I often give this essence when I see people have high standards for themselves—whether it is in their diet, their restrictive personal habits, the unwillingness to experience enjoyment, or even strong self-denial on their spiritual path.

This may also prevent them from asking for help when they need it because they hold themselves to very high standards manifesting in a push to be perfect. Rock Water allows them to release rigidity, become more flexible, and get in touch with feelings that might have been deeply buried. It is also good for those who find that they are not feeling the results from other flower essences.

**Scleranthus:** What kind of decision-maker are you? There are people who tend to vacillate between two choices, sort of like Macbeth—to do or not to do. Those who vacillate between two options need Scleranthus since this indecision and confusion can be draining and exhausting.

**Star of Bethlehem:** The six-pointed Star of Bethlehem releases the trauma and grief of the past so that you start to move forward. It soothes and provides a sense of comfort and is one of the most important remedies in the flower essence repertoire, bringing balance and calm when you have faced a shock of some kind—accidents, disappointments, etc. If you are caught up in the swirling white water of trauma in the past or in the present and perhaps even numbed it out, this essence can help. Star of Bethlehem is also one of the essences in Rescue Remedy or Five Flower Formula.

**Sunflower:** This essence helps you maintain your center without getting drawn into the dramas that play out around you. With it, you can stay calm rather than react instinctively. The Sunflower essence helps us to appreciate our own value while allowing us to recognize the gifts and contributions of others around us. You can learn to feel good about yourself without needing attention or validation, helping you balance self-love without pride or arrogance.

You can just be! When you step into your power, you don't just take space—you fill it! In the presence of sunflowers, I learned everything grows a little bigger. Allowing yourself to be seen is Sunflower essence.

**Sweet Chestnut:** When I hear the words, "I can't take it anymore" or "I'm at the end of my rope," or any other signs that someone has reached the limits of their endurance, it's a call for Sweet Chestnut. This is the essence for feeling that you have reached your breaking point when your anguish feels unbearable, bottomless, and endless. Sweet Chestnut lifts the burden of this suffering. This was the last of the essences that Dr. Edward Bach discovered, healing what has often been referred to as the "dark night of the soul." Just as the massive, deep roots of the sweet chestnut tree give birth to mighty trunks and branches covered with flowers, this essence responds to the cry for help as if from the depths of Mother Earth herself, providing courage and faith.

**Vine:** Often people who need Vine can become selfish, imposing their will on others. They need to be in control and can be dominating, authoritative, and controlling—overriding other people's opinions, being proud, and demanding complete obedience. Sometimes, this tendency can be seen in a parent who dominates the home with a lot of discipline. While Vine personalities can be good at leadership and organizational tasks, these gifts can become subverted into control and power over others. This essence shifts this need to control others to becoming more tolerant of other opinions, inspiring others by helping them to know themselves and find their own path.

**Walnut:** This essence gives you the strength to break away from the limiting influence of past experiences, constricting beliefs, and outmoded values of a community. This essence can help by disrupting control by a dominant or forceful personality or family. It helps you in making changes by giving you the courage to follow the call of your destiny, protecting you from being oversensitive to outside influences in the midst of such shifts. Walnut gives you the strength to pursue your dreams, end or begin relationships, make career changes, and even with transitions relating to birth and death. This essence is the remedy that breaks the link and frees you from the "spell" of the past. It allows you to persevere despite the objections and ridicule of people around you. It gives you the strength to follow your own inner voice.

**Water Violet:** This essence helps us enter the matrix of human relationships with warmth by sharing ourselves with others. Such people may prefer to work alone, do not share their feelings, and can be quite self-contained. From a limp handshake to unfriendly body language, there are many conscious or unconscious signals that may make us appear aloof, unfriendly, proud, or reserved. Water Violet essence helps you appreciate social relationships, enter into them with warmth, and offer advice without becoming too involved in the affairs of others. Water Violet opens up the capacity to being with other people.

**Wild Oat:** This essence is the remedy for uncertainty. If you are wondering what to do, add two drops of Wild Oat for direction. Clarify your ambitions, find your purpose, create specific steps for success: wouldn't you love to do that? Clarity and direction come from our inner realm, not the outer world. Wild Oat is the flower essence when you are uncertain of your path forward, giving you the inner guidance to move in the direction of your soul's desire. Try this essence for at least a week and if you wish, journal the thoughts that come up.

**Wild Rose:** I often give my clients Wild Rose when I notice there is an apathy or disinterest in activities and in life, and when they seem resigned to their life and lack the will or effort to improve their circumstances, or are unable to find joy or to access the passions they once had. According to Dr. Bach, they have "surrendered to the struggle of life without complaint." This might be the result of a long illness or if someone has been through a long bout of challenges, depleting their vitality and interest in the world around them. According to Julian Barnard, in his book, *Bach Flower Remedies: Form and Function*, with this essence, a person will "keep working at a problem until it is solved." The Wild Rose flower essence restores an interest in life and a connection to the physical body and physical world. You can also pair Wild Rose with Mustard or Gorse to restore optimism, interest, and joy in life. While you will find yourself doing things enthusiastically, completing tasks at hand, the shift is so subtle that it's easy to miss.

**Willow:** Willow flower essence helps us let go of resentment and replace it with acceptance, forgiveness, and gratitude. When we feel others are to blame for our situation or circumstances, we are filled with bitterness and negativity, and it's hard for us to move forward in this state of mind. The essence of Willow picks us up when we feel life is not fair, when we are drowning in self-pity and sorrow. We might look at our life in terms of its success markers or accomplishments—the job, the promotion, the house, the partner, and even our weight—making us resentful of others who seem to have it all or at least what we want to have. Willow helps us take responsibility for ourselves, let go of victimhood, and resentment toward others, and life itself so that we can flow with it.

# Resources

## Order Flower Essences

Most essences are available online. I usually buy the Bach Flower Remedies online or from a natural health store near me. I also buy these remedies under the Healing Herbs brand through Flower Essence Services: fesflowers.com.

You can buy the starter kit mentioned in Appendix C on page 246 (7.5 ml/0.25 fl oz) through the fesflowers.com website and a dosage bottle to begin. You can also buy the larger sizes of the Bach Flower Remedies (20 ml/0.7 fl oz) online or at a retailer near you—bachremedies.com/en-us/where-to-buy/.

## Books

There are plenty of books available on flower essences.

*Flower Essence Repertory* by Patricia Kaminski and Richard Katz is a description of the Bach remedies and those created at Terra Flora. It is also an exhaustive cross-reference of the emotional states the remedies address.

- store.fesflowers.com/publications/flower-essence
  -repertory/flower-essence-repertory.html

Stefan Ball, director of The Bach Centre in England, is the author of several books on the remedies and oversees the Center's education programs.

There is also Dr. Edward Bach's original writing, which is now combined into *The Essential Writings of Dr. Edward Bach: The Twelve Healers and Heal Thyself*:

- amazon.com/Essential-Writings-Dr-Edward-Bach/dp/ 0091906725/ref=tmm_pap_swatch_0?_encoding =UTF8&qid=&sr=

or

- bookshop.org/books/the-essential-writings-of-dr -edward-bach-the-twelve-healers-and-other -remedies-heal-thyself/9780091906726

Download your mini workbook that will help you identify the source of your current blocks, with visuals to inspire you to create your own altar:

**healyourancestralroots.com/workbook**

# List of Exercises

**Chapter One: Why Heal Your Roots?**

Journal Exercises     42

**Chapter Four: Discovering Family Energy Fields**

Journal Exercises     91

**Chapter Five: Healing with Flower Essences**

Identify Your Emotions Exercise     108

**Chapter Seven: Rewriting Your Parental Story**

Healing through Visualization     147

Journal Exercises     148

Flower Essences     148

**Chapter Eight: Parents Give and You Receive**

Journal Exercises     166

Visualization Exercise     166

Altar Exercise     167

Release Your Parental Triggers     168

Flower Essences     168

**Chapter Nine: Everyone Belongs in a Family**

Journal Exercises     181

Prayer     183

Altars     183

Family Discussion     184

Flower Essences     184

## Chapter Ten: The Path Back to Yourself

| | |
|---|---|
| Journal Exercises | 199 |
| Animal Symbolism Exercise | 199 |
| Synchronicity Exercise | 200 |
| Flower Essences: An Optimism Formula | 200 |

## Chapter Eleven: Connecting with Mother Earth

| | |
|---|---|
| Walking Meditation Exercise | 211 |
| Connecting to Water Exercise | 212 |
| Flower Essences | 213 |

## Chapter Twelve: Let Your Life Blossom

| | |
|---|---|
| Journal Exercises | 224 |
| A Mind Map Exercise | 226 |
| Flower Essences | 228 |

# Acknowledgments

Infinite grace and support appeared in many ways. There were so many people who helped me find my way forward. To all of them, I am deeply thankful. They are my soul tribe.

I am indebted to Richard Katz and Patricia Kaminksi, who started me on the journey of the flowers and allowed me to experience the wonder of Terra Flora, and to my mentors, Beth O'Boyle and Nancy Buono, Bach flower educator for North America. I am deeply grateful to Beth for reading this manuscript and continuing to share her wisdom and guidance on the flowers with infinite patience. Linda Maratea has been an invaluable part of my journey with the flowers for years, and I am also grateful to Rebecca Dawn for all that I have learned from her.

Words are inadequate for expressing my gratitude to Archana Mehrish, for reading the manuscript, giving her feedback, and for being my fellow traveler in the field of flower essences, ancestral healing, and more than that—for just being in my family field.

Dan Booth Cohen and Emily Blefeld taught me so much about family constellations, sharing their wisdom and insights with compassion and grace, helping me trust my intuition and flap my wings. Thank you for bringing so much magic into my life! Lori Wells, Aitabé Fornés, Freedom Cartwright, and Jean Papagni: you live in my heart. I am especially fortunate to have participated in workshops and classes with Susan Ulfelder of the Hellinger Institute of DC, and Mark Wolynn: each masterful teachers in their own right.

From jumbled thoughts in the original manuscript to a coherent final product are many hands that are almost invisible. Mary Carroll Moore—thank you for your tremendous patience and support over the years as these ideas took shape. Nancy Peske helped me sharpen and clarify what I wanted to say with her sage advice and insights that went far beyond this book. You have helped me travel further than I could ever imagine. Bev West forced me to think about all the things that I wanted to avoid saying. I see your hand in so much now. And last but not the least, my editor, Jennifer Taylor, thank you for rolling up your sleeves and digging into what would make a coherent manuscript. This book would not have been a reality without you. You helped me make it over the finish line!

I am deeply grateful to my clients who trusted me enough to be a part of their healing journey. However, even though the stories in this book are true, the details and names have been altered so that they are not identifiable. Some of them are composite stories for the sake of readability. I would like to thank Alia Malek for providing research assistance for this book, and Queenie Verhoeven for her unflagging administrative support.

Joyce Tattelman, you have been an integral part of my journey for the past two decades. Kavitha Buggana, Toni Carbone, Colette Donahue, Hilde Fossen, Arun Gowri, Jerry Kantor, Jen Karofsky, Soni Masur, Katherine McHugh, Robin Richardson, Donna Trabucco, Dot Walsh, and Kelly Wingo—thank you for so many heartfelt and insightful conversations that have shaped this book. Maggie Sky gave me spiritual shelter and office space at Roots and Wings when I needed it. A big thank you to Jenna

Soard—may your light shine as you help people birth their magic and purpose into the world.

My beautiful circle of friends in all the places I have lived—you will never know how much each of you has filled me and nurtured me. I am grateful to have had you in my life. Even when sometimes the threads of daily connection are lost, the ties continue to live in me. For my friends in Boston, you fill my days with nourishing walks, meaningful conversations, delicious celebrations, and reasons to dance the night away.

I feel that I have been blessed to have in my life—Nandini Bhatia, Ajay Chowdhury, Jayanto Chowdhury, Mika Chowdhury, Aarti Dayal, Sharmila Dayal, Kiran Gera, Nam Menon, Babi and Tina Nobis, Kirti Pande, and Ashok, Sadhana, and Meghan Pasricha. I am forever indebted to my sister Brinda Prakash who has always been my biggest cheerleader, my pillar, and my support, as well as my fun-loving, effervescent brother-in-law Vipul, and my beloved nephew Viraj. You mean so much to me and always will. Through all the ups and downs of writing this book, my husband, Ranjay, has been by my side supporting and encouraging me when all I wanted to do was give up. Wherever our life journeys continue to take us, I will always be grateful that you were by my side. I could never have made it this far without you. And to my beloved children, Varoun and Shivani—I hope that one day you may read this book and find in it perhaps answers that you may seek.

# Index

## A

*aarti,* 209
All Saints' Day, 111
All Souls' Day, 111
altar, 49, 91, 113–18, 167, 175,
    177–78, 183–84, 189, 198,
    275, 278
  altar exercise, 167, 275
Anandamayi Ma, 54
ancestral altars, 8, 41, 112, 114,
    116, 118, 139
Angel's Trumpet, 113, 256
animal symbolism exercise,
    199-200, 276
ashram, 53, 55–56, 60
astrologers, 50–51, 195
*atta,* 47

## B

Baby Blue Eyes, 149, 169,
    247, 256
Bach, 35, 97–100, 104, 108,
    269, 273
  Edward, 96, 98, 271, 278
  essences, 96, 97, 99
Bach Flower Remedies, 100,
    246, 273, 277

Ball, Stefan, 98
Barnard, Julian, 100
Beretvas, Tasha, 220
Blefeld, Emily, 78, 79
Boszormenyi-Nagy, Ivan,
    131, 211
Boundaries Formula, 250
Bowlby, John, 135
brandy, 95, 169, 244, 268
Buddha, 65, 115, 146, 163
Buddhism, 39
Buddhist Goddess, 146, 210
Buttercup, 104, 229, 251,
    257, 264

## C

Calla Lily, 229, 252, 257
Catholicism, 146
Centaury, 97, 250, 258
Cerato, 253, 258
Chakra Bible, 166
chakras, 72, 99, 107–8, 115
Chestnut Bud, 185, 247, 259
Chicory, 103, 148, 247, 251,
    255, 259–60
Chinese medicine, 64, 66–67
Chopra, Deepak, 193

Cohen, Dan, 78, 79, 142
Confucius, 160
Crab Apple, 104, 185, 229, 251, 260–61

**D**
deities, 49, 114, 118, 146
Devi, Lila, 100
Direction Formula, 253
*diyas,* 59
druids, 266

**E**
Echinacea, 268
Emoto, Masaru, 209–210
empath, 250, 267
entanglement, 178
essential oils, 9, 18, 96, 98, 113, 244–45, 262

**F**
family constellations, 11, 79, 82–85, 87–90, 103, 119, 216, 221, 279
family constellation therapy, 12, 36–37, 78–80, 85, 89, 91, 133, 145, 194, 224, 282
family curse, 30, 176
father archetypes, 146
Fireweed, 268
Five Flower Formula, 241, 246, 268–70
Foor, Daniel, 89, 113

**G**
Gorse, 97, 200, 249, 261–62, 273

Green Bells, 262
Green Cross Gentian, 262, 268
Green Nicotiana, 262
Green Rein Orchid, 262
grounded, 205-7

**H**
Hanuman, 46, 195-96
Hellinger, Bert, 79
Holly, 148, 167, 184, 247, 254, 263
Holocaust's Long Reach, 84
*Homeopathic World,* 35
Honeysuckle, 105, 149, 213, 255, 263
honoring ancestors, 111–12
Hornbeam, 213, 263

**I**
Impatiens, 201, 263–64, 269
Indian masters, 118, 141
    mythology, 164
    philosophy, 160
    teachers, 39, 60
Iroquois, 39
Islam, 160

**J**
journaling, 41, 246
Jung, Carl, 28

**K**
Kaminksi, Patricia, 69, 264, 266, 277, 279
Kaminski & Katz, 256
Kantor, Jerry, 161, 236, 280

karma, 9, 43, 45, 89–91, 141,
    171, 190, 195, 259
karmic plane, 218
Katz, Richard, 69, 264, 277, 279
Kierkegaard, Søren, 193
Kundalini yoga, 180
Kwan Yin, 115, 146, 210

L
Larch, 265
Lehrner, Amy, 171
Letting Go Formula, 254
Lourdes, 100, 209

M
Macaulay, Lord Thomas
    Babington, 56, 57
Macbeth, 252, 270
Mariposa Lily, 149, 169
Maslow, Abraham, 219
Maugham, Somerset, 44
Meaney, Michael J., 134
Mercier, Patricia, 166
Mimulus, 35, 66, 102, 104, 229,
    254, 265
mind map exercise, 226-28
Mother Earth, 9, 202–13, 262,
    271, 276
Mother Teresa, 257
Mustard, 35, 66, 149, 250,
    266, 273

N
Native Americans, 181, 183, 209
Neff, Kristen, 220
nightmares, recurring, 171

O
Optimism Formula, 249

P
Paramhansa Yogananda, 54
Patterns
    emotional, 28, 37, 85,
        138, 236
    karmic, 119, 236
Paul, Margaret, 220
Pert, Candace, 32
Pine essence, 267
Pink Monkeyflower, 229,
    252, 267
Pink Yarrow, 169, 250, 267
Pitr dosh, 110
Pomegranate, 100
PTSD, 149
pushkar, 209

Q
Queen of Strengths, 151

R
Rakoff, Vivian, 84
Ram, archetypal Eastern
    hero, 196
Red Chestnut, 185, 251, 268, 269
Rescue Remedy, 106, 241,
    246, 269–70
rin, 128
    matr, 128
    pitr, 128
Rock Water, 100, 212,
    252, 269–70
Rock Water essence, 212

**S**

*sadhu*, 46–47

Saint Shirdi Sai, 46

*samadhi*, 224

*Sani*, 195

Saturn, 195

Sbarra, David, 220

Scleranthus, 106, 253, 270

self-compassion, 9, 166, 218, 220, 237

self-love, 9, 166, 169, 189, 229, 251

Self-Worth Formula, 9, 169, 229, 254

Seligman, Martin, 34, 135

Sitka Spruce, 262

St. Just, Anngwn, 165

Star of Bethlehem, 149, 169, 269–70

Sunflower, 270-71

Sweet Chestnut, 149, 169, 184, 200, 249, 271

Synchrodestiny, 193

synchronicity, 28, 121, 190, 192–94, 198, 200, 218

synchronicity exercise, 200, 276

**T**

Talmud, 160

*tarpanam*, 8, 120-24, 183, 291

Terra Flora, 68–71, 80, 95–98, 100, 277, 279

*thali*, 47, 53

Thich Nhat Hanh, 202

**U**

unconscious loyalties, 8, 139, 141, 221–22, 231–32, 237

**V**

Vaillant, George, 151, 152, 153, 164

Villoldo, Alberto, 112, 114–16

visualization, 146-147, 166-167, 275

**W**

walking meditation exercise, 211, 276

Walnut, 228, 248, 250, 253, 272

Water Violet, 272

Wild Oat, 106, 185, 228–29, 253, 259, 272–73

Willow, 100, 105, 148, 167, 201, 248, 254, 273–74

Wolynn, Mark, 136, 165, 171, 172, 280

**Y**

Yehuda, Rachel, 171

Yerkes National Primate Research Center, 170

Yosemite, 204

**Z**

Zulus, 79

# About the Author

**Anuradha Dayal-Gulati** is a certified energy practitioner specializing in ancestral and emotional healing. A transplant from India, she came to the US to earn her Ph.D., in economics. After fifteen years in finance and academia, she left it to learn how to help people create the life they want.

Even though she had a resume of accomplishments, degrees, and professional experience, none of these helped her when she entered the "dark night of the soul." Discovering flower essences—a way to shift emotions—and drawing on her spiritual heritage gave her the power to see her choices with clarity and courage, abandon her career, and craft a life in alignment with what she truly believed. Her training in ancestral healing work and experiences with family constellation therapy allowed her to see repetitive patterns that appeared in her life and her clients' lives and learn how to release them.

For the last decade, she has been working with clients to help them release the past, reclaim their personal power, and come home to harmony and themselves. By learning to tune into their emotional guidance system, they find the inner confidence to create the lives they want. For Anu Dayal-Gulati, the work she does is not just another job. She has found her calling.

She lives in Boston, MA, with her husband and two children.

To learn more about Anuradha Dayal-Gulati's
work, her services, and her workshops,
visit **healyourancestralroots.com**.

FINDHORN PRESS

# Life-Changing Books

Learn more about us and our books at

**www.findhornpress.com**

For information on the Findhorn Foundation:

**www.findhorn.org**